MW01699939

MICRO-COMPUTERS

THE BUSINESS SERIES FOR OWNER/MANAGERS

MICRO-COMPUTERS

MAKING TECHNOLOGY WORK FOR YOUR BUSINESS

H. Denman Lawrenson, C.A., Ronn Lepage, C.A., Paul Sullivan

Deloitte & Touche

KEY PORTER BOOKS

Copyright © 1990 by Deloitte & Touche

All rights reserved. No part of this work covered by the copyrights hereon may be reproduced or used in any form or by any means – graphic, electronic or mechanical, including photocopying, recording, taping or information storage and retrieval systems – without the prior written permission of the publisher.

Canadian Cataloguing in Publication Data

Main entry under title:
Microcomputers

(Small business series)
ISBN 1-55013-158-3

1. Business – Data processing. 2. Computers.
I. Deloitte & Touche.
II. Title: Guide to computers.
III. Series: Small business series (Toronto, Ont.)

HF5548.2.D45 1990 658′.05 C89-090762-5

Key Porter Books Limited
70 The Esplanade
Toronto, Ontario
M5E 1R2

Typesetting: Southam Business Information and Communications Group Inc.

Printed and bound in Canada

90 91 92 93 94 95 6 5 4 3 2 1

Contents

ACKNOWLEDGEMENTS

Microcomputers: Making Technology Work for Your Business was written and produced with the help of the authors' colleagues at Deloitte & Touche: Arlene Anholt, Signe Ball, Ron Dimon, Robin Kissack, Franca Lauro, Kevin Moon, Stuart McKelvie and Rick Sullivan. The invaluable editorial work of Ed Bishop is greatly appreciated.

PREFACE

This book represents a significant departure from past books on microcomputers. Instead of merely listing and describing the options that are presently available, like a computer catalogue with explanatory notes, and leaving you to figure out what items are appropriate, it focuses on managing the introduction of computers in the workplace. It is aimed, in particular, at the individual who either owns or manages an independent business. Owner-managers are now almost universally aware that computers can streamline routine operations, improve efficiency and increase profitability, but many continue to be wary of the pitfalls that await the non-expert approaching computerization for the first time. With this person in mind, this book takes a look at all aspects of computerization and demonstrates how a comprehensive plan can virtually eliminate risk and ensure a smooth transition to computerized operations.

As the experience of many business people in the last ten years demonstrated, investment in computers cannot, and should not, be seen as a static, one-time decision, in which needs are identified and problems solved once and for all. Changes within businesses, in the market, in the demands made by regulatory agencies and tax legislation, and the evolution of technology itself must all be taken into account.

The business with limited financial resources will ordinarily spread its capital investment over a period of time. The key to getting the most benefit from staggered expenditures is to establish priorities that are tailored to the needs of the business, and then spend money first where it will do the most good. This means that the objectives of the business – for example, profitability, growth and competitive advantage – must be the point of initiation. The owner-manager should approach computerization, with these objectives in mind, and as a continuing process, to ensure the maximum return on investment, and maximum responsiveness to changing conditions.

Computers do not act in isolation from operators. Their real power and benefit is only realized when the person at the keyboard is properly trained and motivated to push the computer to its limits.

This book is intended to guide the owner-manager through the computerization process. The approaches to computerization it presents are based on hundreds of successful computerization assignments carried out by Deloitte & Touche across Canada in a wide variety of industries and businesses. The examples and cases related in the text are based on the actual experience of our dedicated full-time computer professionals located in over 70 centres across the country. These professional computer consultants have grown with the technology and are leaders in the business application of computers. (Please note that, while the case histories described are drawn from the actual experience of our staff, the names of the companies and individuals involved have been changed.)

We are confident that this book will be useful to you as you make your way through the complexities of computerization, and that in the process, you will be better able to achieve the goals that you have set for yourself and your business.

Introduction

Every day, more and more owners and operators of businesses are turning to microcomputers to help them manage their organizations. And many of these owner-managers are subsequently reporting significant improvements in the way their companies operate.

Consider Jamie White and her brother Mark. When they inherited the family business in 1987, it had a proven track record. So, instead of trying to improve on a good thing, they continued to manage the business as their parents had. But preserving the status quo had its drawbacks. In the first two years of operation, White spent nearly twelve hours a day preparing financial statements and maintaining the company's accounts receivable, accounts payable, and inventory records. To speed things up, she decided to introduce a computerized accounting and management system. Three months later, she still had accurate and up-to-date information about the company's performance, but she also had more time to spend managing and expanding the business.

Morris Siemens had a different problem. Siemens owned an independent tire store in western Canada. A few years ago, he noticed his inventory was gradually growing. He wanted to lower his stock but he didn't want to lose sales. So he invested in an automated inventory control system that was able to assist in determining optimum inventory levels. A year later, sales were up slightly and his total investment in inventory had been slashed by 20 percent.

Jerry Blake installed a computer to record each item sold in his Vancouver men's clothing store. He had become concerned that although the amount he sold remained fairly consistent, his profits were shrinking. The computerized system allowed Blake to assess the profits he made on each sale. On the basis of this information, he decided to pay his staff a sales commission on the gross margin he made on their sales rather than the volume of sales. In a short time, his employees raised company profits to their former level.

Dino Rosetti, the owner and manager of an independent pizza parlour in Hamilton, Ontario, had a different purpose in mind when he introduced his computer system. Rosetti discovered that by distributing flyers and coupons he could entice more customers into his small establishment. But the cost of producing these promotional materials was higher than he could afford. So Rosetti invested in a desktop publishing system, which allowed him to produce attractive flyers and brochures quickly and cheaply. Before long, more customers were eating his pizzas, and his sales revenues were up.

These are just a few of the many success stories told by owner-managers across the country. Still, although most owner-managers are aware of the gains to be made by investing in technology, the majority have yet to take the plunge. How long they can wait is a question each owner-manager must answer individually. But it's a question that must be decided soon. Since only one or two of every five small businesses manages to survive more than six years, today's owner-managed businesses need the competitive advantage computers were created to provide. To remain profitable, businesses need tools to assist them with planning and cash management. To monitor the results of their actions, they need timely and accurate financial information. Computers can provide all this and more.

Today, computers are no longer too expensive or sophisticated for the average owner-managed business. The lower prices for hardware and the new, easier-to-use software make this a great time to invest in a computerized system. But before setting out, there are some things an owner-manager needs to know. Whether considering purchasing the company's first computer, or expanding the present system, he or she needs to think of computerization as a process.

This book outlines a strategy for the successful implementation of a computer system. It is aimed at first-time buyers who are thinking of introducing computers into their organizations and at owner-managers who have already purchased a computer but feel they aren't getting full value from their systems.

For more than 125 years Deloitte & Touche, a leader in Canadian business, has been helping owner-managers develop the strategies they need to remain competitive. Our experience as one of Canada's foremost accounting firms has helped us understand how businesses operate. Over the years, with more and more companies automating their accounting procedures, we have also had to develop expertise in the area of computer technology and understand ways computers can be used to help owner-managers make their organizations more profitable. The strategy presented in this book has been used successfully by hundreds of owner-managers across the country to introduce computer technology to their businesses.

Denman Lawrenson, national director of management consulting services for Deloitte & Touche, points out that a strategic approach to computerization significantly reduces the owner-manager's risk of failure: "Current literature indicates less than 50 percent of computer software is ever fully utilized. By using the principles outlined in this book, our owner-managed business clients have achieved a success rate of more than 95 percent."

Our strategy is broken down into three sections. The first part, Chapters 1 to 4, will help you decide whether you even need a computer and if you do, what areas of your business should be computerized. These chapters will also assist you in identifying the right system for your needs. The second part, Chapters 5 to 7, addresses the problem of getting the system running. Issues discussed include training, maintenance, support, and conversion. In the last section, Chapter 8 discusses how to use a consultant if you need help with the computerization process, and Chapter 9 provides information on how to go about estimating costs.

1 / Thinking About Computerization

One of the keys to success in any business is planning. A well developed plan can guide your business through enormous changes.

A successful southern Ontario publishing company began as a one-person operation carried out in the owner's garage. Everything was done manually by the owner, except the preparation of copy, which was sent out to a professional typesetter. As the business prospered over the next ten years, the owner gradually automated the production process, first introducing word processing equipment and then adding automated typesetting equipment. The staff also grew, and so did the need for sharing information. To help the production department communicate with the editorial staff, the owner linked the word processing and typesetting systems. The departments could then swap revised copy back and forth. At the same time, the company's double-digit growth resulted in the expansion of the sales force, the creation of a circulation department, and additional administrative personnel. Each department had to be able to communicate with at least one other department. In all, the business required the addition of three distinct systems, each one capable of being linked to the others. In less than ten years, the company went from a manual system to a fully automated system and from one person to a staff of one hundred employees, each of whom had a computer on his or her desk.

BENEFITS OF PLANNING FOR COMPUTERIZATION

EVOLUTION

The publishing company succeeded because the owner realized that computerization was an evolutionary process that required a plan. Before introducing a computer into your organization, you need a plan that will guide you through the purchase and implementation of a system. This plan should address everything that directly or indirectly relates to the use of computers in your business, from the type of software you buy to deciding which employees should be trained to operate the system. Understanding how a plan works, the various parts involved, and how they relate to one another is almost as important as the content of the plan.

It is helpful to think of the plan as a map designed to help you reach your goal of higher profits or lower costs. Just as you wouldn't drive across Canada to a location you'd never visited before without consulting a road map, bringing a computer into your business demands careful consideration. First, you have to know where you are now and where you want to end up. If you already own a personal computer, your goal may be to put a unit on each worker's desk. Or you may simply want to automate one job function, like word processing or inventory management. You must have a clear destination in mind. The computer plan, like a road map, will help you get there and steer clear of obstacles and costly detours along the way.

ALIGNMENT TO BUSINESS OBJECTIVES

To find areas where a computer can help you to reach your goals, you need to break down your company's operations into component parts and to isolate the various tasks performed by each employee. The next step is to make sure the computer plan and the business objectives of the organization are closely aligned. It's neither necessary nor wise to automate all the tasks once they have been identified. The highest priorities in your business plan should be addressed first in your computer plan. Less critical operations should be assigned a lower priority.

MANAGE EXPECTATIONS

In many organizations, the future users of the computer system have grandiose ideas of what the new equipment will allow them to do. Your computerization plan will help you ensure that your employees have a realistic view of the computer's capabilities. It will also act as a check to make sure you have considered all the implications of implementing a computer in your organization.

COMMUNICATION

Your computerization plan can also be used to explain your intentions to employees and other interested parties, including your accountant and your banker. Having documented all the details of computerization, you'll be able to communicate your intentions with confidence.

PLANNED PURCHASE DECISIONS

Because the computerization plan sets out a clear target for the future, you can plan all computer-related purchases with this goal in mind. Planning your purchase decisions will help you avoid system redundancy by ensuring that hardware and software acquired during the early stages of computerization will harmonize with the long-term plans of the organization. It will also discourage staff from requesting individual systems and computers that do not conform to the overall strategy.

THE INTERRELATIONSHIP OF VARIOUS APPLICATIONS

When developing a computer plan for your organization, consider how the various applications interrelate. For instance, it would be very difficult to implement a desktop publishing system without first introducing a word processing package. Similarly, a point-of-sale system usually relies on the prior implementation of an inventory control system.

TIMING

A schedule is an important part of your plan. By allowing for fluctuations of your business cycle, you will be able to take advantage of slow periods in your organization and to avoid overloads during busier periods.

COST CONTROLS

A part of your computerization plan should be a budget that will help you control the costs of automating your organization. All businesses are limited in the amount of funds that can be invested in computerization, and a good budget will ensure that you get the best value for your money. It will also make sure money is distributed appropriately and spent in the right areas.

FINANCING/CASH FLOW

The cash flow of the business will be affected by the implementation of a computer system. By timing the introduction of the system, the computerization plan will help you work around cash flow problems and ensure that proper financing is in place, if you need it.

THE PARTS OF A COMPUTERIZATION PLAN

Now that you are familiar with the benefits of a plan, you can start to formulate your own. We will look at these steps in greater detail in later chapters.

GOALS AND OBJECTIVES

The first step is to set your objectives. What do you expect a computer to do for your organization? What tasks or functions do you expect it to perform? When setting these objectives, it's important to analyze the specific requirements of each area of your business. Only if your software requirements are clearly defined can the best match be made between your needs and the available

SOFTWARE REQUIREMENTS

With your list of goals and requirements in hand, you must next find the software that fills those needs as efficiently as possible. Software refers to computer programs. A program is a series of instructions designed to perform a task. The instructions are normally saved on the computer to be repeated at a later date. In this book we will typically be discussing applications software. Applications software is a program or group of programs designed to solve a specific task – word processing, inventory control, etc. (See Chapter 3.)

HARDWARE AND OPERATING SYSTEM

Computer hardware is the physical part of the computer including the central processing unit (CPU), the monitor, keyboard, and printer. The operating system is special software required to control and manage the processing of programs and respond to users' requests, such as "save a file" or "load a program." After you have identified the right software for your needs, you should investigate available hardware (monitors, keyboards, printers, etc.) and operating systems. There are many options to choose from, and it's important that you understand the differences and how each will affect your business. Above all, you must make sure your hardware and operating system are compatible with your applications software selection. (See Chapter 4.)

EDUCATION AND TRAINING

Training your staff to operate your computer system is critical to the success of your plan. Training will ensure that your staff not only understands the system but also knows how to make use of the computer's full capabilities. Our experience indicates that one day in the classroom is equivalent to five days spent reading the manuals. Education and training also ensure that the features available in the software are applied in an appropriate manner to your business.

Your training plan should identify what specific training is required for each member of your organization. (See Chapter 5.)

CONVERSION

When it comes to computerization, most owner-managers make the mistake of underestimating the time and cost of converting information from the old system to the new system. As a result they end up with an inefficient, underutilized system. Your computerization plan must allow enough time and money to convert from your present system. (See Chapter 6.)

SUPPORT AND MAINTENANCE

Once the initial investment in a computer system is made, don't forget the need for ongoing support and maintenance. You may need to hire an outside firm to solve any software problems your staff encounters. Another company will provide the maintenance necessary to keep your hardware and operating system working. Regular upkeep will ensure that hardware failures or software upgrades are taken care of on an ongoing basis. (See Chapters 7 and 8.)

COST ESTIMATES

Each of these areas – training, converting, support, and maintenance – costs money. You will need to budget accordingly. By making cost estimates ahead of time, you will be able to plan to fit your company's requirements and budget restrictions. (See Chapter 9.)

"CLOSET COMPUTERS"

As consultants, we often come across "closet computers" in owner-managed businesses. These computers were purchased with good intentions but were never properly integrated into the business, usually because too few resources were committed to training and conversion.

That's exactly what happened at L & S Properties. The owners originally set a very tight but realistic budget for the computerization of their business. But on the recommendation of a hardware dealer, they spent more than 80 percent of the budget on expensive equipment. Although they still had sufficient funds left for the purchase of several modules of good accounting software, only a few dollars remained to cover training. Nothing was set aside to pay for outside assistance during the complex process of automating the old manual system. As a result, no one was properly trained to operate the new software. After six months, the staff became so frustrated they reverted to the manual system, and the computer gathered dust on the accountant's desk. In the end, the owners had to spend far more than originally planned to have a consultant come in, restore the system, and get everything running.

With proper planning, these problems can be avoided.

2/The Computerization Plan

An ambulance firm in a mid-sized eastern community had been using computers for some time, but their existing system was antiquated and was not providing the information the firm's management required to run the business. Gerry Wild, the principal owner of the organization, wanted to move from the existing system to a new information system that would meet all management's needs. Wild understood the importance of careful planning and developed a computerization plan for the organization.

He started by reviewing the existing situation and identifying the benefits that new software would provide. These applications were given priorities according to these benefits.

Wild then looked at the company's present hardware and considered the ways that it could meet the new hardware requirements. In this way, he made maximum use of this existing investment.

Next, Wild looked at training requirements. He knew that his staff would have to learn new skills to use the new hardware and software. He analyzed their existing skills, determined what new skills they would need to acquire, and outlined the training required to meet those goals.

Wild then set up a plan to convert his data from the existing system to the new system. To do this, he had to change the way documents such as invoices and reports moved through his business, set up new procedures to ensure all information was accurately entered into the system, and develop written procedures so that staff would have guidelines to follow under the new system.

Wild's system is now producing the information he requires. His staff are very happy with the new challenges presented to them. Many of the tedious tasks they used to perform manually are now done by the computer. We asked Wild how he felt about planning: "We spent a significant amount of time planning and preparing for our transition to the new computer system. Our organization has always been focused on our people. We wanted to make the transition as simple as possible. We feel that computers should be an evolution, not a revolution. Our time spent planning ensured that the transition from the old system to our new system went efficiently and effectively. We now have a system that meets all of our needs, our staff are very happy, and we are in a position to grow from here."

IDENTIFYING THE BENEFITS

Using a computer system to help your business meet its goals and objectives can result in two distinct benefits. There are tangible benefits that lead to direct profits. But there are also significant intangible benefits: computerization can improve the working environment, employee morale, and customer satisfaction as well.

Tangible Benefits

Tangible benefits are easy to identify and measure, since they usually take the following forms:

- Direct cost savings
- Improved sales
- Wider profit margins

Direct cost savings are possible from many areas of your business. When a small manufacturing and distribution organization in western Canada decided to implement a computer system, it did so based on a benefits analysis that projected cost savings in a number of areas, including inventory control. The results were even better than expected. Before automating, the company often stocked items that sold poorly. But with an automated system in place, slow movers were identified and their numbers cut back significantly, reducing inventory levels by $100,000 and saving the company over $10,000 in the first year.

Direct cost savings also result from the better use of labour through automation. In the case just described, automating the accounts receivable system allowed staff to send invoices with shipments and to tighten up credit policies on overdue accounts - tasks they previously had little time to do. Also, by using a computer to print monthly customer statements, the organization saved two days of the accounts receivable clerk's time every month. The clerk used that time to pursue outstanding accounts more aggressively, resulting in a $40,000 reduction in the average outstanding receivables balance.

The second type of tangible benefit computers make possible involves **improved sales**. A men's store recently implemented a computerized customer database. By tracking the types of purchases made by their clients, they were able to contact individuals that would be interested in specific sales items. Sales increased by 8 percent in the first year of operation.

In a manual system, the owner-manager usually doesn't have access to up-to-the-minute sales results. Often she or he has no way of keeping track of what's selling and what isn't until a proper inventory is carried out. A computer system that tracks sales on an ongoing basis can monitor both inventory and sales and display the information immediately. This information can be used to identify how quickly products are moving and can help the owner-manager to maximize profits by making sure best-selling items never go out of stock and that poor-selling products are not reordered too soon.

Computerization can also result in **wider profit margins**, the difference between what an item costs and what it sells for. One company recently enjoyed a 40 percent increase in the margins after bringing a computer on board. Before computerizing, the company paid its salespeople a commission based on volume of sales. As the economy slowed and demand deteriorated, the salespeople were pressured into cutting prices to maintain a consistent sales volume and commission level. As a result, the company's sales remained healthy, but the profit margin dropped significantly. By introducing an automated inventory control, retail invoicing, and order entry system, the owner was able to generate sales margins statistics. Based on this information, she found a way to raise the salespeople's commission percentage by paying on margin rather than units sold. Six months later, sales were down slightly from the previous six months, but margins were up. Salespeople were happier because they were doing better, and the company managed to increase profits.

Margins can also be improved by using a computer to determine optimum pricing. In a fast food restaurant where competition is heated and merchandise is very price-sensitive, the owner needs to know which products are selling and which are not. By monitoring the daily information available from a computerized inventory control and sales analysis system, he or she is in a better position to adjust prices for the best margins.

Every day, one of Canada's leading hardware and automotive retailers generates data to determine optimum pricing. The company's sophisticated merchandising system allows it to predict sales for certain products based on selling price and where they're located in the store. The system is used to rearrange a store's layout each week to maximize margins and sales volumes. Although most small businesses have no need for this level of sophistication, even a small-scale computer system can prove beneficial if it fits the company's objectives.

Intangible Benefits

Although you should decide to computerize only if you expect increased profits or lower operating costs, sometimes it's hard to measure the value of automating your business in dollars and cents. Often, the benefits you *can't* measure prove to be the most significant. It's impossible to put a price tag on the confidence and peace of mind that having access to timely and accurate information gives you. Without such information, too many decisions rely on guesswork. Also, the detailed information available from the system will allow you to monitor your organization's progress towards its goals and to make necessary adjustments along the way to ensure optimum success.

Improving client satisfaction is another intangible benefit made possible through automation. Here, even small things matter. For example, it's no secret that clients prefer to do business with organizations that exude professionalism. Clearly printed invoices and customer statements instead of handwritten ones make your company look professional. One company that recently implemented an automated invoicing and accounts receivable system used the computer to print short messages on customer invoices and statements advising clients of special products and services it was offering.

BENEFITS ANALYSIS

Identifying all the potential benefits of computers can be a daunting task. To help you get started, this section outlines some typical business applications and the common benefits associated with them. Neither the benefits nor the applications used as examples are meant to be comprehensive. The list is simply intended to demonstrate what you should be looking for when you conduct your own benefits analysis. Use caution to ensure that these examples apply to your needs. Also be sure to add other benefits that apply to your business but are not included in the examples provided.

GENERAL LEDGER AND FINANCIAL REPORTING

Many owner-managed businesses currently use a service bureau to prepare their monthly financial statements. A service bureau is an organization (sometimes your accountant) that charges a fee for doing your monthly bookkeeping. Much of the cost of this service can be eliminated by introducing an automated general ledger system. A general ledger is a composite of all the transactions made by your business, including accounts payable and receivable, inventory, and so on. The general ledger is a financial map of all the business your company conducts and is used by your accountant to create your monthly financial statements. Of course, not all the service bureau costs will be automatically eliminated. For example, if your staff does not have the appropriate training to complete the monthly financial statements, you may wish to have your accountant continue to review bank reconciliations (the balancing of your monthly financial transactions) and finalize monthly statements on your behalf. At the very least, however, an automated ledger system will eliminate many of the costs of entering data in the preparation of your financial statements.

Many small businesses today still subscribe to the "shoe box" approach to accounting. Under this system, anything with a number on it, including receipts, copies of invoices, and cheque stubs, is dumped in a box or envelope and then handed over to an accountant. Often receipts are missing, information is illegible or incomplete, and the accountant has to reconstruct everything that happened to the business in the previous year. This takes time – time the business owner is paying for, and time during which no one knows how the company is doing financially. Much of this time can be saved by having your staff enter all financial information into an automated system as soon as it is received. One of the benefits of computerization can be easily estimated in this case by looking at the monthly service bureau fees and calculating how much that cost would be reduced.

If your business does not now prepare monthly financial statements, you are missing an opportunity to control general and administrative costs. Financial statements are like Polaroid snapshots. They provide an instant portrait of how well you are doing each month. They also allow you to recognize trends in your business's operation. If gross margin is slipping, for example, monthly financial statements will help you find a reason and act on it. Again, it is important to look at the benefits of this information in the context of your organization. Generally, monthly statements allow you to trim 1 to 2 percent from your general and administrative costs through better management because you can better monitor and control your expenses on an ongoing basis.

We all understand the importance of budgeting and planning. We also recognize that budgets are ineffective unless they are closely monitored and compared to actual results. Implementing a good general ledger system will allow you to prepare more detailed and accurate budgets based on the previous year's information and on current plans. By storing last year's information, comparisons can be easily made. Your monthly statements will also help you keep track of how your actual results stack up against your budget. But it is difficult to quantify the benefits of proper budgeting. Look at your operation and compare your actual results to what you expected to achieve. If you find that your business often falls short of its target, proper budgeting and monitoring through automation might help eliminate much of the discrepancy. Whatever you save as a result of accurate budgeting represents the value of the benefit.

An automated general ledger system can also save money on interest charges. If prior to introducing a computer you did not prepare monthly financial statements, your bank may have been charging you a premium on your operating loan because it could not monitor your business. Several companies have reduced the interest rate on their operating loans by providing their bankers with sound, monthly financial information, accurate accounts receivable listings, and up-to-date inventory information. Providing this information not only reduces your banker's risk but it also increases his or her confidence in your ability to manage your business.

If you presently prepare monthly financial information using a manual general ledger, you'll know how much time is involved in making sure all the details are included and all the data is accurate. That time can be significantly reduced with a computerized system. In addition, since data have to be entered only once, rather than many times over as in a manual system, the new system can dramatically reduce errors caused by incorrectly entered figures.

Table 2.1 will help you quantify the benefits of an automated general ledger system for your organization.

Table 2.1 Benefit Analysis – General Ledger

How much money will you save by introducing a general ledger package?

	Monthly Benefit
1. How much will it eliminate or reduce your service bureau costs? (Give actual service bureau costs.)	$________
2. How much will it reduce general and administration expense through better management? (Estimate 1 to 2% of monthly general and administration)	________
3. How much improvement do you expect to see in your business's performance as a result of better budgeting and monitoring? (Estimate.)	________
4. How much will you save from improved interest rates on your operating loan? (Calculate the reduction in rate/12 × average monthly outstanding balance.)	________
5. How much will you save by reducing the time spent on manual preparation of monthly financial information? (___ hours/month × $___/hour.)	________
6. Other ____________________	________
7. Other ____________________	________
TOTAL MONTHLY BENEFITS	$________

ACCOUNTS RECEIVABLE

Few businesses operate on a strictly cash basis. Credit is a fact of life today, but extending credit to customers can create administrative difficulties, especially when it comes to collecting outstanding payments. A computerized accounts receivable system offers many benefits; the most significant is the reduction in the amount of time spent preparing monthly statements. Many businesses spend up to three days every month manually preparing regular customer statements. These monthly invoices are so time-consuming, some companies choose not to bother with them. This decision, however, can lead to difficulties since most people pay their accounts only when the bill arrives each month. An automated system can greatly reduce the time spent on monthly statements and can give your staff the opportunity to concentrate on collections.

Many businesses also refrain from calculating and tracking interest charges on overdue accounts because of the time-consuming paperwork involved. With a computerized system, such calculations are essentially automatic, requiring very little time or effort. Because no labour costs are involved in calculating these charges, everything you collect represents a direct savings, which by itself may be enough to justify the purchase of a computer for your business.

Accounts receivable are one of your organization's most liquid assets. An error made in entering figures or a change not made to a client's account will result in lost income. Such mistakes are common in a manual system, where amounts must be transferred, in some cases by hand, to a customer's account. A properly controlled accounts receivable system should eliminate any errors resulting from manual posting by automatically transferring the invoiced amount to the customer's statement file in the computer. True, it is difficult to quantify how much you save by reducing the chance of these errors, but bear in mind that mistakes can translate into increased paperwork and decreased customer confidence. All errors are costly; some just come with larger price tags. When calculating the benefits of an automated accounts receivable system, these costs should be seriously evaluated.

As mentioned earlier, an automated system will also allow you to print sales messages on the bottom of your monthly statements. Such messages are effective marketing tools, since invoices and monthly statements are often handled by key decision-makers in client organizations. The benefits you might gain from this advertising are intangible because it is hard to predict customer response. (However, once instituted, this system can be monitored to find out how many sales leads are either directly or indirectly generated.)

Managing cash flow is important in any small business. The faster outstanding accounts are collected, the less money you need to borrow to operate your business, and the more you have to invest. You need accurate and reliable information to ensure that you are not inadvertently caught short. By providing you with the information you need to track the average collection time for each of your customers, a computerized system will permit you to predict cash receipts in a reasonably accurate manner and to time your payroll to coincide with periods of high cash flow. If you do come up short, knowing when money is coming makes it easier to persuade the bank to extend your line of credit.

Finally, the availability of up-to-date information will allow you to handle customer inquiries effectively. If a client calls with a question about a bill, being able to respond immediately demonstrates your company's credibility. Your customers' confidence in your organization will grow, resulting in the quicker collection of outstanding accounts. Table 2.2 will help you quantify the benefits of computerizing your in-house accounts receivable system.

Table 2.2 Benefit Analysis – Accounts Receivable

How much money will you save by introducing an accounts receivable package?

	Monthly Benefits
1. How much will you save by reducing the time you spend preparing monthly financial statements? (Allow ___ hours X $___/hour.)	$__________
2. How much income can you generate from finance charges? (Multiply interest rate by % collected.)	__________
3. How much will you save when you have better control over accounts receivable to ensure all invoices are posted and collected? (Estimate.)	__________
4. How much will your sales increase from advertising on customer statements? (Estimate.)	__________
5. How much will better cash management save you? (Multiply the reduction in outstanding accounts receivable by the interest rate/12.)	__________
6. How much will you gain from better client service? (Estimate.)	__________
7. Other ______________________________ ______________________________ ______________________________	__________
TOTAL MONTHLY BENEFITS	$__________

ACCOUNTS PAYABLE

Collecting money on outstanding accounts is only one side of the coin. The other is accounts payable. Most businesses not only extend credit, they also receive it from suppliers, banks, landlords – anyone whose goods or services they purchase to help run a business. Paying these accounts requires just as much management as receivables does. The most significant savings related to accounts payable often come from the accounting area, where the time spent preparing cheques and posting payments to the general ledger is often reduced. Computerized cheque writing, for example, can automatically record in your general ledger the amount paid to each supplier, eliminating the need to keep track of what you have and haven't paid. When quantifying this benefit, estimate the amount of time you currently spend recording invoices and payments and calculate how much will be eliminated through computerization.

An automated accounts payable system will also put an owner-manager in a better position to capture discounts available from suppliers. Most suppliers, for example, offer a discount for prompt payment. Many also charge interest on the unpaid amount after a specified period. A computerized system will provide you with your available discounts, your operating loan and your cash position to determine whether or not you should take certain discounts.

The key to successful cash management in any organization involves the careful monitoring of accounts payable. Small businesses have to know exactly how much money they owe over the next 30 to 90 days, especially if they're using a line of credit. For instance, if your records indicate that you owe a total of $25,000 to your insurance company, your landlord, and your suppliers by the end of the month and you expect to have only $15,000 in the bank, you can plan to have your line of credit extended, or make arrangements with your suppliers to delay payment without any interruption in service. A good accounts payable system will provide you with detailed reports projecting cash requirements and will allow you to monitor cash flows more closely and time your business cycle accordingly. By reducing your operating loans, you will improve your profitability. Table 2.3 helps you quantify the benefits of an accounts payable system.

Table 2.3 Benefit Analysis – Accounts Payable

How much money will you save by introducing an accounts payable package?

	Monthly Benefit
1. How much will you save by reducing the time spent on manual preparation of payments and posting to the general ledger? (Figure ___ hours saved/month X $___/hour.)	$__________
2. How much will you save by being able to capture supplier's discounts? (Estimate.)	__________
3. How much will improved monitoring of cash flow save you? (Estimate.)	__________
4. Other ______________________________ ______________________________ ______________________________	__________
5. Other ______________________________ ______________________________ ______________________________	__________
TOTAL MONTHLY BENEFITS	$__________

RETAIL INVOICING

In many distribution organizations that prepare invoices manually, bills are often sent out as much as a month or more after the goods are shipped. A computerized system can eliminate this lag by producing an invoice at the same time the order is taken. In many cases, the invoice will accompany the shipment allowing the customer to begin the payment process much earlier in your cycle. Not having to prepare invoices manually also saves your staff time, giving them the freedom to pursue outstanding accounts receivable or concentrate on improving cash flow.

By letting you compare the cost of an item with its selling price and by monitoring the quantity sold, computerized retail invoicing allows you to produce daily sales and margin analyses calculated by product and by salesperson. This vital information will help you decide what products to carry, what commissions to pay, which salespeople are producing, and so on. As well, by tying invoicing into the inventory system, product levels can be closely monitored.

Finally, a computerized retail invoicing system will let you balance your cash receipts much faster, providing you with better control over the proceeds. For example, cash registers can be checked more regularly than the usual once a day, providing more detailed information on cash discrepancies. Although in most cases this information does not lead to a significant cost saving, it does free up your senior employees or managers who would normally spend time on these tasks. With an automated retail invoicing system, these employees are free to concentrate on more profitable activities. Table 2.4 will help you quantify the benefits of a computerized accounting system.

Table 2.4 Benefit Analysis – Retail Invoicing

How much money will you save by introducing a retail invoicing package?

	Monthly Benefit
1. How much will you save by reducing the billing cycle? (Multiply days reduction/365 by interest rate/12.)	$________
2. How much improvement do you expect to see in your business by having better sales information? (Estimate.)	________
3. How much will your revenue increase because better quality invoices increase customer confidence? (Estimate.)	________
4. How much improved margin do you expect from paying salespeople commission on margin? (Multiply increase in margin by average monthly sales.)	________
5. How much will you save with quicker daily cashouts? (Figure ___ hours saved/day × $___/hour.)	________
6. Other ____________________	________
7. Other ____________________	________
TOTAL MONTHLY BENEFITS	$________

INVENTORY CONTROL

You can benefit from a computerized inventory control system in many ways, some of which have already been discussed. Obviously, it can help you control the level of your inventory. A proper system should give management the opportunity to reduce the number of times an item goes out of stock and to lower the quantity of slow-moving products. Better inventory management in turn translates into increased sales revenues and reduced carrying costs, because you are stocking only items that are in demand.

In most owner-managed businesses, knowing the exact value of inventory is the key to determining profitability. To determine this value in a manual system, stock has to be counted regularly – a task that is both time-consuming and prone to costly errors. A computerized system will reduce the number of times you have to count your stock. It will also reduce the amount of time spent physically counting and pricing your stock. By using bin locations, which identify exactly where particular items are located, physical count sheets can be arranged to coincide with the layout of the warehouse. This plan helps reduce time spent looking for inventory and physically counting what is on hand. When calculating the benefits related to an automated inventory system, determine how much time your staff spends conducting a physical count and a pricing of that count.

Sophisticated inventory control systems can provide you with information to determine the minimum level of inventory you should have on hand. The system can be used to prepare a suggested order list for your purchasing department when inventory drops below a particular level. This built-in warning system can help reduce stock shortages and can greatly assist the purchasing department when it comes time to reorder stock.

Good inventory control systems will also contain names of suppliers and alternative suppliers to assist you during the purchasing process. Alternative supplier information is useful in the event of a stock shortage, and it will give your purchasing department the opportunity to shop around for the best deal.

One of the most significant benefits of an inventory control system in a retail or wholesale distribution organization, where the amount of inventory on hand is usually quite high, is the information it provides concerning the location of available stock.

Finally, many inventory control systems will allow you to print bin and item labels when goods are received. This time-saving feature will create a more organized warehouse, which will in turn lead to reduced costs. Table 2.5 will help you quantify the benefits of a computerized inventory control system.

Table 2.5 Benefit Analysis – Inventory Control

How much money will you save by introducing an inventory control package?

	Monthly Benefit
1. How much will you save with reduced inventory levels? (Multiply reduction in level by carrying costs.)	$____________
2. How much will you save by reducing the time spent on physical inventory counts and pricing? (Figure ___ hours saved × $___/hour.)	____________
3. How much will you save with improved efficiency in your purchasing process? (Figure ___ hours saved × $___/hour.)	____________
4. How much will you gain by reducing stock outs? (Estimate.)	____________
5. How much will you save by being able to print bin and item labels? (Allow ___ hours saved × $___/hour.)	____________
6. Other ______________________________ ______________________________ ______________________________	____________
7. Other ______________________________ ______________________________ ______________________________	____________
TOTAL MONTHLY BENEFITS	$____________

WORD PROCESSING

Word processing is probably the most popular application for microcomputers today. Instead of writing reports, memos, letters, and notes on paper using a pen, pencil, or typewriter, word processing packages allow you to create your documents on the computer screen. Once finished, the document can be permanently stored in a computer readable form, copied or altered in any way. If a mistake is found, the user can enter the correction without having to start over again from scratch. Even if major changes are required, similar procedures can be followed. A physical document, or hard copy, can be easily produced.

These are just the basics. Today's word processing packages do much more than these simple correcting and storing functions. Recent innovations now allow you to create documents that incorporate graphics, different styles and sizes of lettering, and multiple columns. Many programs will also let you merge different documents so you can create a new document without having to enter additional information. Let's say you have a list of clients you send promotional material to regularly, and you want to send a personalized form letter. Usually, the list of names and addresses will be stored in another file. It is easy to update this list and use it for more than one purpose. The word processing package should allow you to make as many copies of the letter as there are names in the database. Using a merge feature, the word processor will go into the database and fix a name and address to each of the letters. Instead of typing all the names and addresses, every time a set of letters goes out, you need to do it only once when you create the document. The amount of time saved by this feature alone often justifies the cost.

Word processing packages also include features such as automatic centering, paragraph indenting, underlining and boldface, line drawing for creating boxes, tables, and charts, automatic page numbering, and justification (lining the text up even at both the left and right margins). Most packages also come with built-in dictionaries that identify misspelled words. This feature is intended to help with proofreading, not to replace it.

Selecting a word processing package can require a lot of thought. Ask yourself what your business will be using the package for. Will you be using it for external correspondence or just for internal reports and memos? Do you write reports or proposals that require charts and graphs, or do you need to generate only text? You may find a powerful system that integrates text and graphics completely unnecessary. Perhaps you need only such basic features as those found in a typewriter. One package, for example, is set up to take advantage of a touch-typist's skills, so the eyes never have to search for a key to carry out a command. This particular program is designed for speed. Most programs sacrifice speed for features. Also ask yourself if your needs are likely to change in the future.

How often do your employees have to redo documents when only a slight change is required? If your business deals with a number of standard documents, or if you communicate regularly with customers and potential clients, computerized word processing can help raise productivity levels dramatically. Table 2.6 provides a checklist to help you assess the benefits of word processing to your organization.

Table 2.6 Benefit Analysis – Word Processing Package

How much money will you save and/or earn by introducing a word processing package?

	Monthly Benefits
1. Time saving for secretarial staff when making changes to documents – i.e., correction of errors and editing.	____________
2. Time saving for producing personalized letters using a single form letter.	____________
3. Access to documents by non-secretarial staff to make changes and produce documents.	____________
4. Cost savings of producing flyers and promotional materials in-house.	____________
5. Other ______________________________ ______________________________ ______________________________	____________
TOTAL MONTHLY BENEFITS	$____________

SPREADSHEETS

Spreadsheets are the second most commonly used computer application. Over time, spreadsheet programs like the best-selling Lotus 1-2-3 by Lotus Development Corp. have become more and more sophisticated, allowing users to calculate budgets and keep track of finances. Often referred to as financial modelling packages, spreadsheets are an electronic representation of the ordinary worksheet used by businesses for manual accounting. A spreadsheet is a grid made up of rows and columns. The intersection of a row and column forms a cell. You can store data in each cell. The data can be either a label (characters) or a value (numbers or formulas). A formula in one cell can be based on values in other cells.

In most businesses, spreadsheets save time by combining different sets of figures. A company planning its finances for the remainder of the year would have to gather statistics on sales and inventory, current and projected budget, and profits left after expenses, to name just a few. Using a manual system, all the data would have to be written on fresh sheets of paper. Determining the desired totals would require constant cross-referencing, addition, subtraction, and multiplication. Any change in the numbers would mean the calculations would have to be done over again from the beginning. With a spreadsheet program, users simply transfer the information into appropriate columns. The calculations are done automatically with a simple command. And when one of the figures is changed, the alteration is automatically reflected in the totals.

Besides saving time, spreadsheets allow companies to avoid costly errors in calculation. In a manual system, errors can occur while recopying the figures and while calculating totals. Because spreadsheets don't require figures to be re-entered, there is little chance of putting a decimal in the wrong place or leaving off a digit. Spreadsheets also eliminate the need for repeated calculations. When forecasting budgets and trying to determine optimum margins, error-free calculations can save the small business operator a great deal of money. Not having to re-enter figures every time a new formula is applied also allows businesses to experiment with different financial scenarios, increasing the chances that they will find the ideal mixture.

Table 2.7 provides a checklist to help you assess the benefits of spreadsheets to your organization.

Table 2.7 Benefit Analysis – Spreadsheets

How much money will you save and/or earn by introducing a spreadsheet package?

	Monthly Benefits
1. Time saving for producing budgets and forecasts, making last minute changes and "what if" scenarios.	______
2. Avoiding miscellaneous errors.	______
3. Time saving for performing repeat-type calculations and specify operations:	
______________________	______
______________________	______
______________________	______
______________________	______
4. Other ______________________	______
______________________	______
______________________	______
5. Other ______________________	______
______________________	______
______________________	______
TOTAL MONTHLY BENEFITS	$______

DATABASE PACKAGES

Databases are large amounts of similar information, such as client names and addresses, combined in a common pool. A mailing list is a good example of a database. While a spreadsheet is an electronic version of a worksheet, a database is like a filing cabinet except that retrieval and sorting can be done automatically. When combined with other software programs such as desktop publishing or word processing packages, databases can be used to create alphabetical directories, lists of contacts, indexes, and so on, saving organizations time spent compiling and sorting information.

Information that is used frequently can be stored in databases for easy access. For example, your company may decide to keep a file of client information available to refer to when customers make inquiries. By using a database, a query about an account can be answered immediately, saving you time and giving your customer a feeling of confidence in your organization.

Table 2.8 provides a checklist to help you identify the benefits of using a computerized database.

Table 2.8 Benefit Analysis – Database Packages

How much money will I save and/or earn by introducing a database package?

	Monthly Benefits
1. Time saved for administrative staff maintaining and updating:	
Customer databases	______
Sales contract databases	______
Products and prices databases and catalogues	______
Employer databases	______
Equipment databases	______
Other ______	______
______	______
______	______
2. Other ______	______
______	______
______	______
3. Other ______	______
______	______
______	______
TOTAL MONTHLY BENEFITS	$______

DATA COMMUNICATIONS

Data communications packages have become much more affordable lately. These packages allow data to be shared by two or more users. In the past, only large corporations such as banks, airline reservation companies, and stock brokerage firms could afford to use data communications. Now, using a simple device called a modem (which allows information to be sent over phone lines from one computer to another) and inexpensive communications software, even small companies can afford to share data.

Small and medium-sized companies usually share data in two manners: internally and externally. In the first, data is shared within the company from one computer to another. Here, information taken from a database, for example, may be stored in one computer and brought to another computer to create mailing lists, address labels, and so on. Any information that must be shared or monitored within a company, such as accounting data, marketing contacts, sales leads, and inventory control information, can be accessed by all employees using an internal communications system. The most common method of sharing information internally is to connect all the computers in a local area network (LAN). A LAN is a physical link joining computer workstations. Basically, these links let the computers talk to each other and pass information back and forth.

The second way data communications can share information is by gathering external information. Databases such as news services, bibliographic research services, credit card checking or verification, and current stock market quotes can all be accessed by using a modem, the most common method for external computer communications.

Generally, computers can help companies make better use of their hardware and software investments by reducing the time spent on researching and on passing information along. A lawyer, for example, no longer has to hire someone to pick up documents or perform information searches. Those searches can be done by modem, or by local area network if there is an appropriate database located within the organization. In most companies, immediate access to information is a benefit that cannot be measured in dollars and cents. Table 2.9 will help you determine the possible benefits of a data communications package.

Table 2.9 Benefit Analysis – Data Communications

How much money will I save and/or earn by introducing data communications?

	Monthly Benefits
1. Uploading/downloading changes for management reports, etc.	________
2. Inventory sharing between locations – therefore lower inventory levels (reduction in inventory and carrying costs).	________
3. Sharing of customer credit data within and between branches to minimize losses.	________
4. Effective sharing of time sensitive management information.	________
5. More timely access to external data sources.	________
6. Reduction in courier/mail costs due to direct data connections.	________
7. Other ________________	________
________________	
________________	
8. Other ________________	________
________________	________
________________	
TOTAL MONTHLY BENEFITS	$________

DESKTOP PUBLISHING

The special needs of many small business owners are met by desktop publishing (DTP) software. Relatively new to the microcomputer market, DTP packages combine text and graphics, using applications traditionally available only to professional typesetters and printers. The software is increasingly being used by companies that print their own flyers, advertisements, posters, brochures, and newsletters. Small businesses in particular have benefited from the desktop publishing revolution, since the software allows them to create their documents within the organization. Not only does this process save typesetting costs, it cuts down the time it takes to finish a project. Having all phases of production take place in-house gives the company more control over scheduling and eliminates many steps leading up to the creation of the final document.

Apart from saving time and money, DTP programs offer other benefits. Instead of sending ordinary letters that won't get read to a mailing list of clients, companies can create striking documents that grab their customers' attention. Professional-looking documents can enhance a company's image, making it seem more competent and professional. Table 2.10 will help you identify some of the possible benefits of a desktop publishing package.

Table 2.10 Benefit Analysis – Desktop Publishing

How much money will I save and/or earn by introducing desktop publishing?

	Monthly Benefits
1. Reduction of outside layout and typesetting costs.	______
2. Easier turnaround time of promotional material.	______
3. Improved business from better image.	______
4. Improved cost recovery from more timely/accurate price catalogues (if desktop publishing is integrated with product database).	______
5. Other ______	______
6. Other ______	______
TOTAL MONTHLY BENEFITS	$______

GRAPHICS

Graphics packages make it possible for computers to create charts and graphs on paper, slides, overheads, and transparencies for sales presentations, lectures, reports, and group discussions. Graphics software often works with other common computer applications, such as word processing, spreadsheets, and financial statement preparation programs. By working with these packages, graphics software can automatically generate pictorial representations of figures referred to. With a spreadsheet, graphics allow financial information to be displayed as a pie chart or bar graph that is easy to comprehend. Graphics packages can also produce charts and graphs to accompany word processing text, improving the look and readability of the document. These qualities are extremely important if your objective is to increase business by producing stunning, professional proposals, reports, and other documents. Sales presentations can also be enhanced dramatically, indirectly leading to increased profits.

When calculating the benefits of computerized graphics, determine how much more successful your documents and slide shows will be. Will you be producing more presentations in the future? Do you want your material to generate more questions from your audience, more sales leads, more contracts? How much does it cost you to produce slide shows? All these factors can help demonstrate direct benefits from computerized graphics.

Table 2.11 will help you identify some of the benefits to your organization.

Table 2.11 Benefit Analysis – Graphics

How much money will I save and/or earn by introducing graphics?

	Monthly Benefits
1. Amount saved on outside costs by in-house production of:	
Slides	
Overheads	________
Graphics for proposals	________
Graphics for promotional material	________
Other ____________________	________
	________

2. Time saved through in-house production of:
   Slides __________
   Overheads __________
   Graphics for proposals __________
   Graphics for promotional material __________
   Other ____________________ __________

3. Other ____________________ __________
   ____
   ____

4. Other ____________________ __________
   ____________________ __________
   ____________________ __________

TOTAL MONTHLY BENEFITS $__________

General Considerations

The examples in this chapter are only a few of the applications of computerization. Numerous applications remain that might prove beneficial to your organization. Once you have reviewed all of the appropriate applications, the next step is to rank each one in order of its importance to your business. For example, if the automation of your accounts receivable system is likely to produce the most benefits, its importance should be reflected in your computerization plan. By quantifying the benefits in this manner, you'll be certain not to automate applications that can promise neither tangible nor intangible rewards and to ensure that those with the most benefits are given priority.

3/Understanding Your Software Requirements

ALWAYS LOOK AT SOFTWARE FIRST

Because the software you choose will perform the tasks that run your business, choosing the correct package is vital. Without it, your computer will be unable to meet the needs of your business. In fact, the most common reason owner-managers fail in their attempts to bring computers into their organizations is that they chose the wrong software. It is therefore essential that before you look at hardware you decide which software satisfies your business requirements. Selecting the software first will also ensure that your system is capable of delivering the benefits identified in Chapter 2.

Far too many businesses underestimate the importance of software. Because hardware is so much more expensive than most software packages on the market, many owner-managers are convinced that the majority of costs associated with computerization are hardware related. In reality, software, training, and implementation make up at least half the initial startup costs. Some industry experts even claim that hardware should account for as little as 20 percent of the total cost. No matter how you look at it, software is much more important to your business than the misleading price tag might indicate. The less thought you put into selecting the right software package, the less chance you'll have of reaping the benefits of a computerized system. This chapter will help you analyze your needs to make sure you select the best software package possible.

How to Select the Right Software

The data-processing industry and the consulting profession have developed a process to help you select the appropriate software for your business. Over the years, that process has become more and more refined, and questionnaires can now pinpoint key business requirements. For the majority of owner-managed businesses, a simplified version of the process is all that's required, especially now that most hardware and software packages are available from retailers. The following steps will guide you through the process of successfully choosing the right software solution:

- Define your needs.
- Compare your defined needs to available software products.
- Select the most appropriate software based on closest fit, price, and other considerations.

Define Your Needs

Defining the needs of your business may seem like a simple task but the process is one of the most difficult parts of the computerization plan. You have to understand your business from top to bottom, making sure nothing is forgotten when you switch over to an automated system. An error here could mean the difference between success and failure. For example, your inventory control system may identify items by their part number, the suppliers' part number, and an assigned stock-keeping unit (SKU). The different systems of identification are important if you need to access information directly on the computer and run reports based on the different identification codes. If a customer calls asking about a particular item and has only the manufacturer's part number, your chances of making a sale are much better if you can answer your customer's inquiry immediately. But if your system won't let you access your inventory records by manufacturer's part number, you'll have to spend time physically searching for the information. By the time you find the answer, the customer may have tired of waiting and gone off to a competitor.

Because the assessment of your needs is such a formidable undertaking, this chapter includes a series of checklists to show you what to look for in the areas of general ledger, accounts payable, accounts receivable, inventory control, and retail invoicing. General business software for applications like word processing and spreadsheets has not been included in the checklists. Although it's important to examine your needs before making a decision, most leading software contains all the features and capabilities your company will likely require. Your decision here will have a less direct impact on your business than the accounting package you choose.

Each series of checklists is broken down into five main areas that must be addressed before you purchase a software package:

System Capacity. Will the software allow you to handle the volume and size requirements of your business, such as long account numbers and large dollar amounts?

System capacity refers to the ability of the software to handle all necessary transactions and tasks in the frequency, manner, and format you require. Your software selection will have to handle the volume of your business, including things like number of transactions per period and their dollar value, the business's overall revenue, and the number of employees. Depending on the application you're reviewing, capacity constraints could involve size (for example, the number of accounts you handle, or the number of transactions you perform per month) or numeric limits. In this section of the checklist, you will identify the number of transactions or master file records your business requires. Master files are permanent records, such as a customer's accounts receivable master file, which contains name and address information, customer number, credit limit, and account balance. By comparison, a transaction file contains all those transactions that affect a customer's balance in a master file. If your business generates a large number of transactions per customer, your software package must have the capacity to accommodate the high volume.

Stored Information. What information do you want to save for processing, analysis, and reporting?

The structure of the software will determine the information that is available to your organization. The software you choose should be capable of retaining all the information that is critical to your operation. If you will be recording supplier information, you may have to record both a telephone number and a facsimile machine number. Make sure the master files have room for this extra insertion. When completing this section of the checklists, consider the amount and kind of information that is currently used and stored in your business. Your current needs will help identify the information you want to store.

Processing Capabilities. Is the system capable of handling all the required transactions and calculations?

The processing capabilities of software are the functions it will perform. Let's say, for example, that you want to be able to analyze how much of the outstanding balance in a customer's account is past due in four time periods, ranging from zero to 90 days. Not all software packages permit this function. In selecting software, pay particular attention to calculations that are unique to your business or industry, such as paying sales commissions based on margin rather than volume. When reviewing the checklist, determine the types of processes currently taking place in your business and identify which ones should be automated. Remember to consider all the tasks performed from start to finish.

Screen Query. Will the information that can be called up onto the computer screen suit your needs, or will hard copy reports be required?

Screen query refers to information that can be viewed on the video display terminal. You may want to be able to access such information as customer accounts, inventory status of a particular item, or sales forecasts for a specific product category. Since the information available through these screens varies greatly from one software package to the other, it is crucial that you know what your needs are. Let's say you require a customer's credit history in order to authorize a transaction. Depending on the software, you may have to print a full report rather than being able simply to call this information up on the screen.

Printed Reports. Will the quality and quantity of reports meet your needs?

The printed reports generated by your computer are the most visible product of the accounting system. They're the only physical evidence you'll have that the software is working. A variety of reports – such as product availability, dollar value of unfilled orders, and revenue expenses compared to revenue forecasts – will be used regularly throughout your company to make management decisions, provide financial information to government, bankers, and other interested organizations, and to plan long-term strategy. The software you select must be able to produce the reports you need to guide and manage your business.

As you fill in each of the checklists, indicate whether the needs specified in each of the five categories listed above are mandatory or desirable.

Mandatory needs are those your operation cannot do without. If you use telephone numbers to identify client accounts, for example, the software must be able to accommodate a ten-digit code. Or if you operate a construction company where monthly invoices often contain holdbacks, or portions of the bill that go unpaid by clients until several months later, the software package you choose must be able to recognize this procedure.

Desirable features, however, are not essential to day-to-day operations, although they offer significant benefits. When identifying these needs, rank their desirability from one to three, with three representing the most desirable.

Compare Your Needs to Available Products

Determining which of the numerous software packages on the market best matches your needs is a formidable task, requiring a great deal of research. The more you know about the products available, the greater your chance of selecting a package that's right for you. This doesn't mean you have to devote yourself to the lifelong study of accounting and business software. Information on the capabilities of various packages is readily available from a number of sources, including dealers, software developers, manuals, magazines, and technical literature, as well as other users and independent consultants.

Each source has its advantages and disadvantages. Some dealers, for instance, are extremely knowledgeable, while others lack the technical background and understanding necessary to suggest the right package for your particular business needs. Salespeople who make exaggerated claims for their software should be avoided. Truly knowledgeable dealers also understand the weaknesses of their products and are willing to discuss them. If your salesperson can't competently discuss a competitor's program, or if technical specifications sound like a foreign language on your agent's tongue, you're not likely to obtain useful information. Also avoid salespeople who don't bother to ask you about your business, since that's the only way they can suggest the right software solution for you. Dealers are particularly useful when you've narrowed your decision to a number of packages and you want to know the advantages of each.

Software developers, on the other hand, can point out the many features and benefits of their products. However, they often lack the objectivity needed to recommend a competitor's product if it represents a superior solution. Marketing literature produced by developers is also a good source of information, but only a thorough review of the software program and manual can cover all the ground. Study marketing literature for a new product from an unknown developer carefully, and confirm the advertised capabilities through an additional source.

Manuals are another source of information. Some developers and dealers will lend you a user manual and a copy of the software on a trial basis, although not all packages are available for this kind of review. Your dealer should at least be able to demonstrate the package for you with sample data from a fictitious company. Generally, the demonstration gives just a brief glimpse of a program's features and capabilities. It's only meant to give you a feel for the products. Nevertheless, you should never purchase a new product unless you've seen it demonstrated.

Other users can also offer helpful information. However, be sure to talk to users from your industry. Many businesses make the mistake of purchasing software on the recommendation of a friend or colleague, or on the basis of its popularity. Although popularity is often a good way to determine a product's ability to adapt to different business needs, the fact that a particular software package runs well in a shoe store is no guarantee that it will be as useful in an auto dealership. On the other hand, newer, less popular products that haven't been thoroughly tested don't usually have a well-documented track record. Research these packages thoroughly before you make your selection.

An independent consultant who knows software well and understands your accounting needs can provide excellent advice on the capabilities of particular software. But a word of warning: a consultant's services can be expensive. You have to decide if the costs outweigh the risks of not seeking expert advice.

Finally, additional information is available through the major computer magazines sold in most bookstores. These publications regularly print comparisons and ratings of popular software packages, including accounting programs, spreadsheets, word processing, graphics, desktop publishing, and so on.

Many sources of information are available to help you select a software package. But, as you can see, they all have their drawbacks and their advantages. The best approach is to use as many of these sources as possible, taking into consideration the limitations and biases of each source.

Selecting the Best Software

Once you've defined your needs and reviewed the available software solutions, you should be in a position to select a software package. This decision should be based on the following set of criteria.

First, consider the **degree to which the software fits your**

organization's needs. Are all mandatory needs covered? If several packages all fulfil the basic requirements, refer to the desired features to break the tie.

Next, consider the following six additional points:

- **Ease of use**. Is the system easy to learn? Does it use menus and clear messages to assist the operator? How easy is the package to implement? How long will it take to get the system running? How long will it take to create the initial data files? Also consider the quality of the manual. Is the user manual complete, accurate and easy to understand. Most software has the manual built in so that you can obtain help at the touch of a key. This is called on-line help. You must determine the quality of on-line help. Does the system anticipate likely choices based on particular situations, or does it simply fill the screen with information for you to read through? Are the instructions easy to understand?
- **Vendor reputation**. Is the vendor an established developer of software and committed to supporting the products? How many copies of the program have been installed to date? How long has the package existed?
- **Availability of training and support**. Does the software dealer or developer offer good technical support? Are training materials available? At what cost?
- **Operating system requirements**. Does the software operate on a commonly used and supported operating system like MS-DOS, Unix, or OS/2?
- **Ease of integration**. Can information be shared? For example, can spreadsheets, databases, and word processing all use the same data?
- **Ability to use pre-printed forms**. Can the system accommodate the cheques and other forms used by your organization, or do you have to generate forms created by the software?

Price should be the final consideration. Although important, it should have the least influence on your final decision. The difference between a top-quality inventory control package and a low-end package is usually less than three or four hundred dollars. If more of your needs will be met by spending a few more dollars, the extra expense will probably prove to be a bargain. When looking at price, less obvious costs should also be considered. These include:

- **The number of copies of the program you need and the number included in the purchase price**.

- **The vendor's policy regarding local area networks** (many computers connected to share information or hardware). Will one package run on more than one computer?
- **Annual maintenance fees for enhancements** (new features added to the software).
- **Annual costs for software support provided by outside experts.**

SOFTWARE REQUIREMENTS CHECKLIST

The selection process is long and involved. It's also essential. To help you save time and identify your needs as thoroughly as possible, the following section provides sample checklists that will guide you through a needs analysis for five common accounting applications:

- General ledger.
- Accounts payable.
- Accounts receivable.
- Retail invoicing.
- Inventory control.

A review of each checklist is included to help you define the software requirements for your organization.

General Ledger Requirements

The general ledger system is typically the cornerstone of the accounting function. The system processes entries from the various accounting applications – for example, sales entries from accounts receivable, expense distributions from accounts payable, and entries from payroll – and then summarizes these transactions. These summaries then form the basis of most of the company's financial and management accounting reports. Without a good, reliable general ledger package, you risk losing timely and accurate management and financial reporting information. Fortunately, general ledger requirements seldom vary significantly from one organization to another, so the chances are good you'll find a package that meets your business needs.

System Capacity: When reviewing system capacities, be sure to determine the number of accounts each package is capable of handling. Many low-cost accounting systems do not allow you to identify information by department or cost centre. Let's say you need a profit-and-loss statement for each of your company's five locations. A package that does not provide for the identification of sales and expense accounts by location would not help you. Some systems restrict the number of transactions that can be kept over a given period. If your business requires an unusual number of accounting periods, make certain the software package can accommodate the request. Many retail businesses, in fact, use 13 four-week accounting periods in a year instead of the more typical 12 months in a year. Since the 13 periods each have the same number of business days, financial results from one period aren't artificially inflated because of an extra day. If you use this system, choose a package than can accommodate it.

Stored Information: Most general ledger systems contain basic information such as account number, department, description, type, and account balance in their master files. If your system requires budget figures or results from a past period for comparison, your software should be capable of holding this information. Be sure to check for this feature before you buy.

Processing Capabilities: The processing requirements of a general ledger system are fairly simple. Usually, a general ledger keeps track of transactions by account number, department number, and source journal, or by the segment of the accounting system in which they were created. Choose a package that lets you enter transactions only if there is a valid account code and that warns you if transactions have no reference numbers or source journals. Most often, a general ledger that won't permit unbalanced entries is also desirable. Also choose a package with features that will simplify how you enter transactions into the general ledger. For example, being able to create a new account during transaction entry can save you from having to exit the general ledger to enter a new program. Also, look for packages with a simple data-entry process. Some have data-entry screens that carry forward all information from the previous screen in the event that much of the information is the same.

General ledger systems are usually batch controlled, which means transactions are entered in batches that must balance, with all debits equalling credits. You should not consider any system that allows an unbalanced batch, such as a journal entry where debits do not equal credits, to be entered.

Some systems will also handle posting and year-end closing differently than others. Study the software you are considering to make sure you are satisfied with the approach being used for year-end closes. As well, many packages don't make allowances for the consolidation of separate companies. Make sure that a subsidiary's general ledger can be combined with the accounts of the parent company if that feature is appropriate to your organization. If budgeting is of primary importance to your business, make sure current information can be utilized by the general ledger system.

Finally, your processing needs may require you to transfer detailed or summary information into other programs, such as a database or spreadsheet, so further analysis can be performed. Let's say you want to identify and extract all general ledger transactions that affect a particular customer or vendor. Since a general ledger system is not designed to allow this, you have to move the data from another program. Most quality accounting software will allow you to share information among different packages. If the general ledger is the final gathering place for most of the information in your organization, this feature may prove extremely beneficial.

Screen Query: Nearly all general ledger systems have some level of inquiry capability so that you can call account balances and transactions up on the screen. Some packages list all transactions that make up an account balance but won't show the fiscal period into which the transaction was posted, or even the source of the transaction posting. Make sure you can call up all the information you will need.

Printed Reports: Most general ledger systems are also equipped to handle the same standard reports. These include:

- **Chart of accounts**. This gives account number and a description of each account.
- **Trial balance**. This is a listing of account balances showing debits in one column, credits in another, and their balanced totals.
- **General ledger detail**. This lists the transactions according to the source of entry.
- **Transaction listing**. This report indicates the order in which transactions were entered.
- **Audit trails**. This report traces all financial results back to their original source, including the invoice, the person responsible for the expenditure, and so on.

Review the report-generating capabilities of the software you are considering to make sure they cover all your needs. While most packages include some form of financial reporting, there is a great discrepancy in quality between low-cost and more expensive packages. Before settling on a general ledger system, make certain the software can produce the reports you use in your business now, and those you'll require in the future. See Table 1 in the Appendix for a checklist designed to help you select a general ledger package.

Accounts Receivable Requirements

An accounts receivable system maintains a record of how much each customer owes your business and how long each of those amounts has been outstanding. Although most available accounts receivable software meets the basic requirements for the majority of small business operators, there are enough differences among the packages to make selection a difficult process.

System Capacity: Some low-cost systems are limited in the number of customers and transactions they can handle. But more typically the systems support only a fixed number of accounts receivable types and bank accounts in the general ledger. In many cases, a company's general ledger will have a separate account for each type of accounts receivable: trade customers, employees, factory warranty claims, and U.S. and Canadian dollar customer. Check that the software you choose has adequate capacity for your needs.

Stored Information: Most systems can maintain basic information for each customer such as name, address, contact persons, telephone and facsimile machine numbers, and the name of the salesperson assigned to the account. This information is used to prepare mailing lists, to send correspondence and statements, and for follow-up telephone calls on outstanding accounts. If you plan to use your accounts receivable software to help manage your business, additional information capabilities may be essential. You may want your system to maintain information for the following areas:

- Each customer's credit limit.
- Each customer's current and prior year sales volume.
- Each customer's current and prior year gross profit volume.
- The average number of days each customer takes to pay an invoice.

Some software packages on the market offer little flexibility when it comes to letting you select certain features that identify what type of account a customer has. For example, you may want to distinguish between "open item" accounts, where amounts owing are tracked by a specific invoice number, and "balance forward" accounts, which identify only the invoices that make up the amount owing for one month after it is either paid or becomes overdue. Check that the software will store information in ways you will find useful.

Processing Capabilities: More sophisticated accounting software often has built-in processing functions designed to improve the speed and accuracy of entering and processing information. Such features include:

- An on-screen display, which accumulates the total dollar value of invoices entered.
- The ability to recall batches of invoices to be posted on a recurring basis, such as monthly rental charges, which are the same each month.
- The ability to add new customers from the invoice entry system.
- The ability to handle and convert invoices that use foreign currencies.

Screen Query: Another important feature you should consider involves the system's inquiry procedures. If your customers frequently want to know their account balances and which invoices make up the total, you need a system that will let you respond as quickly as possible. All accounts receivable packages have some sort of inquiry function, but not all will meet your level of need. Some, for example, will allow you to view only an outstanding balance but not the unpaid invoices that comprise the outstanding balance.

Printed Reports: Most systems also generate the following standard reports:

- **Aged-trial balance**. This report shows the individual invoice amounts owed by each customer, with totals for each "ageing" category, such as 30, 60, 90, and over 90 days.
- **Customer list**. Usually alphabetic, this list includes each customer's name, address, and phone number.
- **Customer statistics**. This report notes information such as the highest amount of credit a customer has ever been granted, the number of days a customer usually takes to pay a balance, and the average sale per invoice for a customer.
- **Credit limit exception report**. This shows only those customers who have exceeded their credit limits. It notes how much they owe and

for how long.

- **Collection report**. This lists, by account executive or salesperson, the amount of money that each must collect from his or her assigned customers within a certain time.
- **Cash flow projection report**. Using customer payment habits, this report forecasts how much cash will come in during a particular period to satisfy outstanding accounts receivables.

Accounts receivable systems differ widely in their report generating capabilities to generate reports. If your organization must know how much a customer owes in ageing periods other than the normal 30-, 60- and 90-day intervals, make sure your software allows user-specified periods. The quality of information provided in the collection reports is also important if you expect the system to help you collect outstanding accounts. For instance, if the reports fail to show a payment received from a customer because it wasn't applied to an invoice, you could make the mistake of going after the payment, and causing embarrassment to you and the client.

Review the different reports covered by the software to make sure your collection needs will be met. Also check that the package lets you produce monthly customer statements. A surprising number of programs don't meet this basic requirement, and those that do may not be able to duplicate the exact type of statement your organization now uses.

Finally, you may want your accounts receivable system to produce collection letters that remind customers of their past due balances. Or you may want to create mailing labels based on the information in the customer files to stick on file folders or send out promotional literature. Again, this feature is generally provided only by more sophisticated systems. Table 2 in the Appendix provides an accounts receivable checklist to help you select an appropriate package.

Accounts Payable Requirements

An accounts payable system is used to record suppliers' invoices. It also records which invoices require payment by a particular due date and which are eligible for discounts if paid by a certain time. Accounts payable packages vary most significantly in how well they help an organization manage cash flow. Basic packages are designed primarily to track payables and distribute invoices for payment to particular suppliers. Seldom can they be used to manage cash flow. For this feature, buyers have to look to more advanced packages.

System Capacity: System capacity limitations most common to accounts payable software are similar to those found in accounts receivable programs. Both types have a tendency to limit the number of control accounts and the number of bank accounts. For example, a system might not allow you to include both trade and inter-company payables, or both Canadian and U.S. dollars.

Stored Information: Nearly all accounts payable system data files include standard vendor information: each supplier's name, number, address, standard terms of payment, and the day of the month the vendor requires payment. More sophisticated systems allow greater amounts of vendor data to be stored. A record of past purchases, for example, can be useful when negotiating with suppliers, but only more advanced systems provide this feature. Alternate payee information is also useful if your organization is involved with group buying and payments are made to one central organization. For example, a number of small, independent furniture stores spread across Canada may form a buying group to increase their ability to negotiate favourable pricing and payment terms. In this situation, the individual stores order goods and receive shipment from suppliers who then bill the central buying group. The stores pay the buying group and the buying group pays the suppliers using money sent by the store. To let the buying group know which supplier to pay, the individual store must have an accounts payable system that identifies the supplier on the cheque.

Processing Capabilities: Advanced packages also offer several processing features:

- An automatic check for duplicate invoices to make sure the same supplier isn't paid twice.
- An automatic distribution of the amounts paid to general ledger accounts based on account codes set up in the supplier field (eg. the system would know to charge an invoice from Bell Canada to telephone expense).
- The automatic ability to allocate discounts, taxes, freight, and finance charges where needed, thereby saving considerable manual calculation.
- The ability to record cheques written manually during a rush period in the month from which the payment was made.

Different packages offer the most noticeable variation in their cheque processing features. Be sure to review the flexibility and controls available within each system to ensure that the one you select is adequate. Flexibility in cheque processing allows you to pay certain invoices while not paying others, even though they may both be due. A "bank reconciliation" feature, which lets you take all the cheques that come back with the statements and enter them by number into the system, is also useful, especially for companies that write a lot of cheques. Strong accounting controls are important to make sure that payments are accurate and authorized. Other accounting controls to watch for include:

- A forced printing of an audit trail to make sure a hard copy is always available. (The system forces you to print an audit trail before you can move to the next step of processing.)
- An on-screen total to check that all numbers have been entered correctly. (The system provides you with a total of the amounts entered so you can compare the amounts on the original documents.)
- The automatic assignment of individual numbers to each transaction.

These features will help you to ensure that information is correct and that you have an audit trail to help you find the original documents at a later date.

Screen Query: It should be possible for management to gain quick access to invoices and payments by vendor number and name. The software should also allow the user to respond to inquiries from vendors concerning the state of their accounts.

Printed Reports: Most accounts payable systems include the following reports:

- **Vendor list**. An alphabetical listing of all suppliers' names, addresses, telephone numbers, and standard terms of credit.
- **Vendor statistics**. A listing of vendors by vendor number, showing standard discount terms and payments, due dates, the total amount of purchases for the current and prior years, and the dollar value of discounts accepted and missed.
- **Overdue payables listing**. This report shows the amount of overdue invoices payable to vendors.
- **Payables still open, or left unpaid**.
- **Aged cash requirements**. This report shows the amount of cash the business will require during pre-set intervals (two weeks, 30 days,

60 days, etc.).

- **Pre-cheque register**. This report lists all the cheques the system would write if allowed to pay every invoice due on the dates specified by the vendors.
- **Cheque register**. A list of the actual cheques written by the system, showing cheque number, vendor, invoices, and the amount paid.
- **Manual cheque listing**. This report provides the same information as the cheque register for cheques written manually and later entered into the system to clear the corresponding invoices.

Review the format of these reports in each of the accounts payable software packages to make sure your needs are being met. Table 3 in the Appendix provides a checklist to help you get started.

Invoicing Requirements

Invoicing packages are designed to meet the needs of three kinds of business environments. In the first, the retail environment, customers purchase goods over the counter and receive an invoice immediately after they tender cash, cheques, charge cards or store credit account numbers. In the second type of environment, the company receives orders from customers through the mail or by telephone rather than in person. The shipping information given by the client is used to prepare an invoice. Virtually all transactions involve credit. In the third type, the service environment, the primary commodity sold is a service. Invoicing systems for service companies like contractors, lawyers, or accountant offices, usually require a great deal of flexibility.

System Capacity: Different companies require different capabilities from their invoicing systems. One may need to keep a file of products and their prices. This company wouldn't want a system that allowed only a limited number of products to be maintained on file. Similarly, some systems that track each agent's sales and calculate commissions can accommodate only a certain number of individuals. Most organizations will want an invoicing package that can compute both federal and provincial taxes. In some businesses that operate in more than one province, complications can arise, since various items are taxed differently by different provinces. A considerable amount of care must be taken to ensure that your system has the capacity to handle the taxation levels and jurisdictions in which your business operates.

Stored Information: The amount of information a system can retain to help analyze sales is also important, since it is essential that the owner-manager be able to determine the profitability of a product. This information includes sales data based on product, customer, territory, quantity of products sold, and dollar amounts for past and current years.

Processing Capabilities: A good system should also be able to process invoices, credit notes, quotations, layaways and deposits, accounts receivable cash receipts, miscellaneous cash receipts, and miscellaneous cash payments. Since most programs are developed in the U.S., it's also necessary to ensure that the system of your choice is capable of performing the complex tax calculations required for Canadian businesses.

Screen Query: The invoicing system should allow you to call up information normally requested by your customers, such as outstanding account balances, layaways, and prices of items you sell.

Printed Reports: A more sophisticated invoicing system will be able to print the following standard reports:

- **Sales and profit analysis** by product, customer, territory, or salesperson in either detail or summary form.
- **Sales and commission reports** by salesperson.
- **Price lists** for salespeople to use in marking products, giving quotes, and so on.
- **Quotation lists** for prices given to customers.
- **Lists of customers** who have deposited money towards a future purchase.
- **Daily reports**, including a sales "re-cap" and cash drawer log that gives a report of all cash register activity.

See table 4 in the Appendix for a checklist of invoicing requirements.

Inventory Control Requirements

An inventory control system basically keeps track of the quantities and costs of each item carried by your company. The quantities go up when items are received in inventory and go down when items are sold. A good system can also identify items that are low in stock and must be ordered and items that have been ordered by customers.

Although most systems will track day-to-day inventory levels and costs, more sophisticated packages can improve your inventory management by allowing you to order in quantities that economically balance carrying costs with the cost of ordering new products.

System Capacity: When analyzing the system capacity constraints of a particular inventory package, determine the number of sites or locations the program limits you to. Basic systems often allow only one location, while more advanced programs allow as many as 99. Also, you may want your system to maintain various categories of inventory. Some packages monitor only finished goods, those offered for sale to the public, making no provision for work-in-progress and raw materials, which are not offered for sale but are used to create finished goods. A system that maintains all categories requires several control accounts to identify to the general ledger the various product categories, locations or departments being kept in inventory. More sophisticated software has the ability to identify these groups of accounts separately. Other concerns when assessing system capacity include:

- Can alternative items be listed for each product? Alternative units are those products that can be substituted for items that aren't currently in stock.
- Can serial numbers be stored for each item? How many numbers can be stored? This feature is important for tracking warranty information from the manufacturer to the customer and for maintaining quality control.
- At how many levels of assemblies and sub-assemblies can materials be inventoried? Most distributors require only a single level because their products are put together from complete items, such as the components of a stereo system in an electronics store. A manufacturing company, however, requires many levels because most of its finished products represent assemblies that consist of a number of sub-assemblies. It may want to keep inventories of these sub-assemblies.
- How many sales history periods can be recorded? A company may want to retain detailed inventory information for several prior years.

Stored Information: The amount of information stored in the system affects how useful the program will be in helping you manage inventory. Good packages can track quantities of items on hand, on order, committed to customers, reserved, and available. A good system should also maintain reorder information, such as minimum levels below which stock cannot fall, optimum or most cost-effective levels, maximum levels, the amount of time required to receive goods, and the quantity level or point in time at which reordering should commence. In a retail clothing environment, for example, the system has to maintain information on the style, colour, and size of various garments. As well, many organizations require a package that lets them purchase or sell merchandise in varying units of measure: individually, by the dozen, or by the gross. Not all inventory systems offer this flexibility. Nor do they allow several pricing policies to be stored within the system. If your organization uses a sophisticated pricing policy, check this requirement carefully.

Processing Capabilities: When assessing the processing capabilities, there are a number of areas to consider. Look at the method for entering purchase orders and for receiving items on those purchase orders. This feature is especially important since delays in implementing inventory control can often be traced to problems in the purchase/receipts area.

Other processing capabilities you should consider include compatibility with order entry or retail invoicing systems. This capability can greatly reduce the time spent entering information required for shipments. Also, if your organization is involved in assembling items for sale, ensure that the inventory system has an appropriate bill of material assembly system process that automatically tracks items assembled from materials in inventory. Finally, physical inventory counts (stock takes) are one of the most time-consuming aspects of inventory management. To help you streamline the process, the system you select should:

- Prepare inventory worksheets by location according to the order in which the items are stored in that location (picking sequence).
- Have a streamlined input system to enter the results of the physical count.
- Be compatible with hand-held portable stock-taking computers.

Screen Query: Although most of the information used in the inventory control system is usually accessed through hard copy reports, sophisticated packages should maintain adequate inquiry capabilities. These would include the ability to view, at a glance, the quantities on hand of a particular item, the quantity stored at various locations, the quantities that have been committed to customers but haven't yet arrived, the quantities ordered from suppliers that haven't arrived, and the amount of time required to receive goods after placing an order. In particular, ensure that the system you select allows inquiry into prices and quantities on hand based on location.

Printed Reports: When it comes to report-generating capabilities, most inventory control packages offer some or all of the following:

- Item status.
- Item valuation report.
- Overstocked items report.
- Reorder report.
- Slow-moving items report.
- Purchase orders and receipts.
- Transaction history.
- Price lists.
- Margin analysis.
- Mark-up analysis.
- Sales history.
- Summary sales statistics.
- Price change report.
- Turnover analysis.
- Inventory aging report.
- Suggested transfer report.

Once you've determined which of these standard reports you require to help manage your inventory, ensure that the software you choose can satisfy your needs. Table 5 in the Appendix will lead you through a needs analysis to help you select the right inventory control package.

WORKAROUNDS, ADD-INS, AND CUSTOM PROGRAMMING

When buying an accounting system for your business, the most obvious choice is a standard packaged program. Like buying a suit off the rack instead of a tailor-made one, packaged programs offer certain advantages. For one thing, because these programs are manufactured and sold in volume, the purchase cost is fairly low.

Tailor-made programs are a one-of-a-kind item, and you pay for the exclusivity. Also, if you ask someone to make a suit for you, you can't expect to wear it the next day. With off-the-rack products, there are few delays to worry about, and you can try them on first to make sure the fit is right. Also, since pre-packaged programs don't require any in-house programming expertise, you avoid all the management problems related to this function.

If after trying on a number of off-the-shelf products you still can't come up with an appropriate fit, you may have to find another way to satisfy your business's requirements. One alternative is the use of manual procedures to fill whatever gaps you find. These procedures are known as **workarounds** and are commonly used by consultants and more experienced users to fit software into various organizations. With a workaround, you can get software to do a task not originally included in the program. Using a spreadsheet program to enter data and prepare special financial reports, such as departmental comparisons and daily cash receipts, is a good example of a workaround, since the package is originally intended as an electronic financial worksheet.

A second alternative is to purchase **add-in** software that will work with your accounting package. Add-ins allow you to perform functions the main software doesn't include, and are available for most major accounting programs. For example, many word processing packages are designed to be controlled from the keyboard. Some use a keyboard and a device known as a **mouse**, which allows you to execute commands. Generally considered a faster method than the keyboard-only approach, mouse capability can be included in systems lacking the feature with the appropriate add-in package.

However, if neither workarounds nor add-ins solve your problem, you may have to consider getting your software **custom-designed**. The obvious advantage is that you can program a system that will fit the needs of your organization the way a tailor cuts a suit to your exact measurements. Of course, this method is time-consuming and requires extensive technical experience. Your first choice should be to make adjustments to the standard package that most closely fits the needs of your organization. The last resort is to write a complete system from scratch.

To develop custom software, you need a professional programmer. Although the costs may seem huge at the outset, it is worth your while to find someone who is established and experienced. Small, independent programmers often leave their clients with more problems. They may, for example, underestimate the time required to complete the program, not make the documentation and user manuals comprehensible to non-technical personnel, or not adequately test the system before implementation. Pay particular attention to the terms of the contract before signing and make sure the job is finished to your satisfaction.

4/Computer Hardware

Now that you have chosen or designed your business software, most of your hardware requirements will already have been determined. Basically, you will have to purchase a computer that has at least the minimum specifications required by the software. These specifications will include everything from the speed of the computer to the size of the hard drive – even the kind of monitor you use can be dictated by your software. Your choice of software will also in most cases determine the operating system you need. Even though your options are limited, there are enough possible variations to make the selection of hardware and operation system a difficult process. This chapter provides a basic understanding of the many options available.

HARDWARE COMPONENTS

When selecting a computer system for your business, it is easy to become overwhelmed by all the options. At times, settling on any one component can seem like a game of chance. However, computer components all fit into well-defined categories, each with its own specific properties and functions. By defining your needs in terms of their separate functions, you'll be able to narrow down your field of choice. Most computer systems consist of a processor, memory, input devices, output devices, storage devices, and interfaces. These are discussed in detail in the following pages.

Processor

The processor controls the operation of all the other components, including the computer's keyboard, memory, and the video display terminal or screen. It is connected to internal memory for the purpose of executing programs and processing data. When selecting a processor, bear in mind the level of processing speed you require, and the type of software you are going to run.

IBM and IBM-compatible computers (sometimes referred to as clones) typically run on a family of processors manufactured by Intel Corp. of Santa Clara, California. The 8088 processor, which became commercially available in 1979, is used in the PC (IBM's abbreviation for personal computer) and XT class computers. Although popular, this processor cannot run the sophisticated software programs being developed today. The 80286 processor, which is used in AT class computers, offers improved performance over the 8088. Intel's 80386, introduced in 1988, is yet another improvement. It is used in business applications that require high-speed calculations (such as computer-aided design and engineering tasks) or as a server. A server is the computer in a network of computers on which all common information is stored. As it is serving all of the other computers in the network, it should be quite powerful. The Intel 80486 processor is now commercially available and an Intel 80586 is being designed.

Another commonly used processor is the Motorola 68000 series. This processor is used in Apple Macintosh microcomputers and many Unix-based systems.

Historically, the introduction of a new generation of processors creates a price reduction in the previous generation. And since processor chips are continually being updated, this can result in savings, depending on your processing needs. If you require a single computer, you can often get all the power you need at a reasonable cost by purchasing a mid-range processor. When choosing a server, however, it's usually wise to select from the high end, since your application will probably require a high level of performance.

Memory

The processor is usually incapable of accessing information directly from storage devices. Instead, it must move this information into memory. Two types of system memory are used by computers: Read Only Memory (ROM) and Random Access Memory (RAM).

ROM contains certain pre-programmed functions that cannot be changed; hence the term "read only." ROM is also permanent, which means it cannot be erased when the computer is turned off. The computer accesses read-only memory after it is switched on to perform a check of the circuitry and to help start the computer. Generally, ROM comes in the form of a solid-state storage chip programmed at the time of its manufacture.

RAM is a volatile form of memory; its contents are erased when the computer is turned off. It is used to hold information and instructions needed to run the software. It is also used to run other programs such as add-ins, which modify how an application functions, and operating system instructions. RAM size is measured in kilobytes (K). A kilobyte represents 1024 bytes or characters of information. Four kilobytes will hold approximately one typewritten page of information. The size of RAM often affects how a program can be run. Most common application software requires a minimum of 512 K of RAM. Applications designed to run under OS/2 require significantly more RAM. A minimum of 640K is recommended for most accounting applications and business packages running under DOS. Today's systems usually offer at least that, and many offer 1 megabyte (1 MB = 1024 K) of RAM as a standard feature. Before you purchase a unit, it's important to consider the cost of memory expansion for future applications. Buying a machine that features memory expansion can save you from having to purchase a more powerful unit somewhere down the road.

Input Devices

Input devices enter information into the computer in the same way we might use a pen to write a letter. There are two commonly used input devices:

- Keyboard.
- Mouse.

The **keyboard** is the most common device used for inputting information. The arrangement of the keys is usually similar to that of a typewriter. Additional function and movement (cursor) keys complete the keyboard design. When selecting the right keyboard, make sure the layout is comfortable and complete. Items to consider include:

- The placement of the function keys. Many systems arrange the function keys along the top in a single row. Generally, they are easier to find in this location – an important consideration for touch typists.
- The availability and placement of a separate number pad. This pad is useful if you will be using the keyboard to enter numbers into the computer.
- The placement of the cursor movement keys. These keys are used

extensively in some applications and should be very accessible. Look for keyboards with large Enter and Shift keys to make data entry as error-free as possible.

The other common tool for input is the **mouse**. When you drag the mouse across the desk surface, an arrow or similar symbol moves in corresponding fashion across the screen. The mouse is used to activate programs by pointing to the name or symbol of the program or function and clicking a button on the mouse.

Other input devices include touch screen and bar code readers. Touch screen technology uses a special screen that is sensitive to the touch of the operator. By touching the screen to select options or enter information, the operator does not require a keyboard. Touch screen technology is today well accepted. In fact, many commercially available applications use this type of input technology. Bar code readers, for example, are most popular in retail point-of-sale systems. They're used to quickly input coded information, such as the item number and price, using a wand or scanner. With bar code readers, the data doesn't have to be re-entered into the system, saving the operator a great deal of time and reducing the possibility of error.

Output Devices

Output devices allow the computer to communicate or display information to the user. The most important are:

- The screen or video display terminal.
- The printer.

The **screen** or video display terminal (vdt) is an important output device. There are several factors to consider when choosing a computer screen. In addition to physical dimensions such as height, width, and depth, it's important to think of screen size in terms of the amount of information that can be displayed.

Clarity and colour should also be considered. Clarity is affected by the colour used to display the characters and the number of pixels contained on the screen. Short for "picture elements," a pixel is a tiny dot, the smallest unit of measure on the screen. The more dots, the greater the detail of the image displayed. The number of pixels is referred to as screen resolution. Very high resolution screens are required for such detailed applications as drafting and architecture. Colour screens are important in a number of business applications to highlight information and system messages requiring the user's attention.

Printers are another important output device. There are basically two main categories of printers: dot matrix and laser printers. Dot matrix, or impact printers, are commonly referred to as pin printers because the device that creates the actual impression of dots (referred to as the head) is made of pins. There are usually 9, 12, 18, or 24 pins in a head. Laser printers, on the other hand, are non-impact devices. When a sheet of paper passes through the printer, it is exposed to light in the shape of the characters specified in the document. In the same way a photocopier takes a picture of the document, the printer applies toner to the areas indicated by the light.

Nine-pin printers represent the lowest offering in the dot matrix category. Because they have few pins, the quality of the letters is generally poor. Twenty-four-pin printers usually produce better results. Laser printers are far superior at printing text and graphics such as charts, graphs, even pictures. Twenty-four-pin dot matrix printers also offer high-quality output for both text and graphics, although they can't match the levels attained by laser printers.

When it comes to using different paper sizes, only dot matrix printers offer a wide variety of choice. Most laser printers are limited to standard-sized paper. Many laser printers come with a manual paper-feeding tray that can be adjusted to accommodate envelopes and address labels. Dot matrix printers often have adjustable paper-feeding guides that can print paper ranging in size from 8.5 to 15 inches wide. There is virtually no limit to the length of paper these printers can accommodate.

Depending on the business application, one type of printer is usually preferable to another. Low-end dot matrix printers, for example, are often used to generate draft-quality reports. If your business needs to create multi-part forms, dot matrix printers are better, since laser printers cannot print multi-part forms and would have to print multiple copies of each document. If quality of type is an important issue, and you intend to use your printer for correspondence, a laser printer is probably the best solution. If your company produces a large number of proposals and reports requiring charts and other graphic images, a laser printer is a must.

Storage Devices

Information and software programs are always stored on some sort of holding device. Four kinds of devices commonly available are diskettes, hard disks, tape drives, and optical disk drives.

A **diskette** is an inexpensive, simple form of removable storage and has the advantage of being easily transportable. It is made of a thin piece of flexible plastic covered with a protective sleeve. Diskettes store information magnetically on the surface of the plastic. When the diskette is placed in the diskette drive, it rotates within the protective sleeve. Information is read from or written on the disk as it passes over special devices, called read/write heads, inside the drive.

The 5.25 inch diskette was the previous standard and is still used by many computers. The new 3.5 inch diskette is more durable and is quickly becoming the accepted standard. Diskettes commonly hold between 360,000 and 1.4 million characters of information – or 90 to 350 pages – although new technology continues to raise the capacity of 3.5 inch diskettes to as many as 20 million characters. The larger-capacity diskettes (regardless of their physical size) are double-density, double-sided floppies, that pack more than twice the storage capacity into the same space. To use the larger-capacity diskettes, the computer must be equipped with the appropriate disk drive to read that type of diskette. In other words, a 1.4-million-character disk drive is needed to read a 1.4-million-character diskette.

Hard drives are similar to diskettes except they have several inflexible platters joined by a spindle – like three or more records on a turntable spaced out vertically. Because they are fixed within a protective covering, hard disks turn much faster than floppy disks, reducing the time it takes to access information. Although smaller and larger disks are available, hard disks currently range between 40 million and 300 million characters – or 40 to 300 megabytes. The hard disk's protected covering also makes it less subject to deterioration over time. Because floppy disks are handled constantly and come in contact with dirt and other destructive elements, they have a relatively short life span. The average hard drive lasts much longer.

Magnetic **tape** cartridges commonly store as much information as hard disks, but they do so in a sequential form. Therefore, specific information cannot be accessed directly; the entire tape must be read to get the last piece of information on it, unlike a diskette, which can be accessed at any point. The more efficient systems, like hard drives, are used to carry out day-to-day information processing. However, sooner or later even large-capacity hard drives get full and it becomes necessary to remove some of the more out-of-date files. Because of their low cost and reasonably high volume, tape storage devices are often used to back up files.

Optical disks, which are like the compact discs used in stereo systems, are another form of storage device. Although access times are somewhat slower than with hard disks, optical disks have a large capacity. In fact, most can store as much as 600 million characters of information. The one drawback is price. Each disk sells for a great deal more than a floppy diskette, while the optical disk reader can cost two to three times as much as a mid-range computer system.

Interfaces

In order for the processor to recognize and run peripheral devices such as printers, modems, optical disk drives, and monitors, these items must be connected to the machine in some manner. The way they are connected is referred to as the interface, or adapter, which is essentially a small port or plug located in the back of the central processing unit. When the cord running from the peripheral is connected to the appropriate port, the processor is able to run the devices.

There are two basic types of computer interfaces: serial and parallel. Serial interfaces are used to send information one piece at a time down a single wire. A parallel interface is used to send many pieces of information simultaneously down a group of wires. A serial interface is comparable to a single lane highway while a parallel interface is similar to an eight lane highway. The RS232C port is an industry standard "serial" interface commonly used in computers. Modems and certain printers are examples of serial devices that require this type of interface. (The RS232 standard is the same type of interface used to connect telephones.) The Centronics interface connects "parallel" devices such as most dot matrix printers. The devices that are attached to the computer dictate the interface required.

The Small Computer System Interface (SCSI) can also be used to connect input and output devices to the computer system. Developed in the early 1980s by IBM, SCSI provides an open (as opposed to proprietary) architecture that can be used to attach and control up to seven peripheral devices, especially hard drives, from one computer expansion slot. This interface allows you to connect formerly incompatible equipment designed by different manufacturers.

Before choosing any hardware, find out what type of interface your peripheral devices require to make sure the system can accommodate them. Keep in mind that computers have a limited supply of available slots. If you require interfaces to several other devices and computers, you may not have enough slots. Make sure there are enough of the kind you need before buying. Also consider possible expansion later on. Sometimes slots are needed to add extra memory or an extra hard drive to your system.

Computer Sizes and Types

Microcomputer systems are available in an astonishing variety of shapes and sizes to suit your needs. There are three common configurations or classes available on the market:

- Desktop/Tower.
- Portable.
- Laptop/Notebook.

The most common type of microcomputer is the **desktop** configuration. In these units, a processor, the disk drives, and the power supplies are contained in one box called the central processing unit (CPU), while the screen and keyboard are separate. The desktop configuration is designed to sit on a desk, the tower configuration is usually kept on the floor.

Portable computers are usually designed with the keyboard, screen, and all other pieces of equipment mounted in a single unit for easy transportation. These portable units typically lack battery power; instead they require an external power source to operate. Although more compact than the desktop version, portable computers are rather heavy and cumbersome.

The third category of computers, the **laptop**, solves the weight and bulk problem of the portable. These units combine all the parts in a single housing and generally come with an internal battery pack so you can use it while in transit. Notebook versions are as light as five pounds and are designed to fit into a briefcase. Laptop and notebook PCs are as powerful as mid-range desktop units.

Of course, there's a limit to how small these computers can become before they can no longer be operated with a traditional keyboard and monitor design. In fact, we've probably reached the limit as far as size is concerned. But as laptops and notebook PCs become more accessible, they're also likely to become more powerful. Areas of technology that manufacturers will continue to address include battery size and power, hard disk storage, and screen resolution.

WHAT AFFECTS THE SPEED OF A COMPUTER?

An important characteristic of a computer is the time it takes to carry out the tasks for which it was purchased. This factor is referred to as the computer's speed or its throughput. If a computer is slow, people must wait for tasks to be completed. Some businesses may find speed less of an issue than others, particularly if the computer is used infrequently or can be left to process information while the operator carries out other jobs. But for many small businesses, speed is an important consideration. Often, a single employee is assigned to a machine for eight hours a day. How productive that person can be is a direct function of the computer's speed. The faster the computer, the more information that can be processed, the more productive the individual becomes. In any case, processing speed should be considered when bringing a computer into your business. Even if your demands are now modest, speed could be an important issue later.

When considering the processing speed of your system, several factors must be considered:

- The amount of data to be read.
- The access speed and transfer speed of the device used to store information.
- The power of the processor chip.
- The speed of the processor chip.
- The number of processors.
- The size of the system "bus."

Unlike the computer, which processes information electronically, storage devices are mechanical, which means they have moving parts. This factor makes them one of the slowest microcomputer components, and means that the amount of data transmitted between the storage device and the computer will significantly affect system throughput. Different programs will handle interaction with the storage device in different ways. For example, a spreadsheet program does not have to interact with the storage device while it's in use, because all the information – the instructions – is in the computer's memory. The speed of the computer will therefore have little effect on how quickly the spreadsheet can be saved and retrieved. A database, however, is too large to be stored entirely in the system memory. It involves the constant transmission of information between the computer's memory and its storage device, making its speed highly dependent on the speed of the storage device.

Since an accounting program is basically a database, bookkeeping packages require faster storage devices. If you have a large volume of data, it's important to know how your software will interact with the storage device. The speed of these devices is usually measured in access time (milliseconds). The lower the access time, the faster the drive. Depending on the application, medium to slow access times may be acceptable. However, for accounting purposes, faster access times are usually necessary.

The power and speed of the processor chip dictates how much data can be processed in a given time and determines the speed at which the computer performs calculations. For example, the Intel 80386 processor chip handles data in pieces that are four times the size of information that can be handled at one time by XT class processors. The 386 can operate at more than six times the speed.

The type of processor chip will often dictate the types of software that can be run on the computer. Some software is designed to run specifically on at least a 286-based processor. As higher-level chips become less expensive, the standard that software developers write programs for continually shifts upwards.

Many computer systems use more than one processor to improve throughput. For instance, by limiting one microprocessor to only mathematical calculations or only video screen management, the main processor chip will have more time to perform other operations, such as running a software program.

"Buses" are the connectors between the processor's memory and other devices on the computer, such as the computer's display screen, keyboard, and storage devices. Higher-resolution screens boasting better graphics-viewing capabilities are continually creating display standards that require a larger processor. A processor that can handle a large amount of information at once but has to interact with a video display screen that handles information only in much smaller chunks will not be able to process to its capacity. In cases like this, the bus that connects the computer's processor with peripheral devices becomes a major bottleneck. IBM's PS/2 series of microcomputers addressed this problem with the introduction of MCA (micro channel architecture) technology, a bus system designed to interact faster and more directly with components that control display terminals, storage devices, keyboards, and printers. An alternative bus technology known as EISA (Extended Industry Standard Architecture – an enhanced version of the older ISA) follows a less direct route when interacting with peripherals.

When selecting microcomputer hardware, keep in mind that one computer may be faster for one type of application but slower for another. Everything depends on the application. If speed is important to your organization, be sure to carry out a trial run and ensure that the hardware you select meets your minimum speed requirements. The following section on operating systems will help you identify the kinds of alternatives open to you.

OPERATING SYSTEMS

Operating systems are support programs that control the operation of equipment and assist application programs. On a very basic level, they act as transparent interfaces between hardware and application software. Operating systems perform such useful functions as letting you know what files you have on disk, allowing you to copy or erase specific files, and telling you how much storage space is taken up on the hard drive by your software programs and data. Generally, the operating system is a collection of programs and instructions that allows you to manage files, run programs, and use devices such as printers, disk drives, and hard disk drives. Most application software is designed to run with one designated operating system. As such, the selection of the software will determine which operating system you can use. The most common operating system is IBM's PC-DOS system – or its alternative, MS-DOS by Microsoft Corp. MS-DOS and PC-DOS have minor differences, but both operate in essentially the same manner and present the same format to the user. Although MS/PC-DOS set the industry standard for many years, it has several limitations. For instance:

- It can access only 640 kilobytes of memory.
- It can be used by only one user and can perform only one task at a time.
- It is unable to use many of the features available in the Intel 80286 processor and more advanced models.

OS/2 represents an alternative to MS-DOS and PC-DOS. OS/2 is an abbreviation of the term "operating system 2" and was developed jointly by IBM and Microsoft. A large and complex operating system, it requires a powerful computer. Minimum requirements for OS/2 include an 80286-based machine, two or three megabytes of RAM, and 40 megabytes of disk capacity.

Apple's Macintosh operating system represents a significant departure from the user interface found in the DOS environment.

Although it provides the same functions as DOS, the Apple Macintosh operating system uses a desktop metaphor, that is, the computer screen represents the top of a desk. It places icons on the desktop to represent objects the user may want to manipulate, such as a sheet of paper to represent a file, a file folder to represent a directory that contains a number of related documents, a disk to represent a collection of software programs, and so on. Basically mouse-driven, the Macintosh operating system creates a stable, consistent environment that most people find very easy to understand and master. Because all Macintosh applications are written in a similar manner, large corporations using the Macintosh operating system save on training time. Unix, developed by Bell Laboratories in the early 1970s, is a multi-user, multi-tasking operating system that until 1980 was primarily used in universities and research departments. Multi-tasking means that Unix – and its many derivatives such as Xenix, AIX, and others – allows microcomputers to run more than one program at a time. For example, while the computer is carrying out a mail merge (combining addresses from a database with a form letter created in word processing), the user could be working on a spreadsheet. (OS/2 is also a multi-tasking operating system. DOS and the Macintosh environment are both single-task systems.) A multi-user environment simply means that more than one person can process information using the same computer. Most versions of Unix allow you to run Unix and DOS applications simultaneously and to switch from one to the other.

LOCAL AREA NETWORKS

In their most basic form, local area networks (LANs) are groups of two or more microcomputers connected for the purpose of communicating. That communication can involve sharing data, application programs, and peripheral devices. Owner-managed businesses typically start with a single standalone computer and move to a local area network as the business expands and more people depend on computers to perform the work.

Although a local area network is meant to simplify the process of sharing data, setting up a network is often a complex undertaking. A medium-sized manufacturing company found this out when it attempted to connect its accounting department to the computer system. The company had already automated its accounts ledger, accounts receivable, and accounts payable systems using three computers (one for the accounting manager who maintained the general ledger, and one for each of the two remaining clerks). Even with automation, the department experienced difficulty keeping the general ledger up to date. Since the three computers were standalone units, whenever changes were made to the general ledger (accounts added, deleted, or modified), or whenever journal entries were posted, the new data had to be copied from the general ledger computer to the other two systems. The accounting manager found that, on various occasions, the general ledger information used by the accounts payable clerk differed from that of the accounts receivable clerk. A local area network would eliminate this problem by allowing a single copy of the ledger to be used by all three people in the department.

The owner-manager's first task was to select the components of the network. She had to be sure that what she implemented would be compatible with the existing hardware, DOS operating system, and accounting software. And she had to do this by following a strict budget. With some guidance and advice, the owner-manager first selected the network operating system. Because she felt it was important to go with well-known manufacturers, she chose an industry-standard operating system that was fully supported by the accounting software. The operating system also offered support for up to eight simultaneous users, which would accommodate anticipated growth of the accounting department. Several vendors had even recommended the operating system as an excellent performer, as long as it was used with the right server.

To minimize complications, the owner-manager again decided to go with an industry-standard computer for a server. (Even though selecting a brand-name computer over a clone stretched her capital budget, she felt she would save money on consulting, service, and support farther down the road due to the product's greater reliability.) The owner-manager's vendor helped her configure the system and recommended the appropriate network interface card for the server and each of the workstations. The network interface card was used to physically connect the computers with a cable. Although the cards were compatible with the hardware, they required a type of cable that was more expensive than the owner-manager had anticipated. To stay within the budget, the vendor suggested a more expensive interface card that would allow the use of the twisted-pair cabling used in telephone systems. This meant the owner-manager could use the cabling system already present in her building.

At this point, the owner-manager was set to buy the network. She had selected all the components, ensured that they were compatible and industry standard; she had arranged for staff training; she'd even purchased an add-on piece of software to make her accounting software perform better on the network. At the vendor's suggestion, she also added a back-up unit, even though she hadn't originally budgeted for the purchase. Because she felt comfortable with her vendor and was grateful for his assistance, she agreed to let him assume responsibility for installing the network.

During the installation the vendor noticed a problem. The two accounting clerks occupied the same office and shared one telephone between them. The installation required that each workstation have its own telephone connection. As a result, a cable installer had to be called in to run new cable to the second workstation. This delayed the network installation by two weeks, although in the end everything operated properly. The owner-manager is even ready to add another computer to accommodate a new accounts receivable clerk – the latest addition to the growing accounting department.

What You Need to Consider

If your business is thinking of setting up a local area network, be prepared for "jargon shock." LANS are incredibly complex systems of computer communications that even in their simplest form can prove difficult to understand. But as long as you learn some of the basic terms – enough to know, for example, that the consultant or vendor is talking about cabling set-ups when the word "topology" is thrown at you – understanding LAN technology will be much easier. Bear in mind, however, that even if you become comfortable with the terminology, you will probably never learn everything there is to know about LANS. Installing a LAN requires a great deal of experience and technical knowledge. In most cases, you'd be well advised to leave most of the technical matters to your vendor or other qualified personnel. The only way to make sure the LAN will work with your application is to have your vendor demonstrate each package before you purchase any kind of networking product. This demonstration is commonly done by testing your application on a network supplied by the vendor or by visiting similar sites referred to you by an expert. If you follow these steps before buying a LAN, chances are your installation will prove successful.

The first thing to do before buying a LAN is to determine whether or not you need one. How many people in your organization share the same information? How dependent are your employees on work completed by others and then passed along? Do files used by the entire office constantly have to be updated? Is there a large database of information, such as customer accounts, that a number of employees have to access at the same time? Answering these questions will help you decide if your business needs a LAN. If you're still in doubt, you can monitor the flow of information and who shares data with whom by tracking the migration of diskettes throughout your organization. Track this migration for a month by having each employee mark down who the disk came from, who it was passed to, and the reason for the transfer. If long lists describing the flow of diskettes are the result of this study, you may have demonstrated a need you otherwise wouldn't have detected.

The most common reason for implementing a local area network is so that more than one user can update and use a single file of information at the same time. This requirement is common in large accounting departments and in order entry and inventory control applications.

Local area networks are also purchased by owner-managers so that more than one individual can use a peripheral device, such as a printer. In many cases, sharing peripherals such as expensive laser printers and plotters can justify the cost required to purchase a quality component, thereby saving money in the long run. (However, if you just want two computers to share a printer, a LAN is probably unnecessary. You can buy a printer switch for this purpose at a much lower cost.) Local area networks are also used so groups of employees can work on common functions such as scheduling, electronic mail (sending messages from one computer to another), and group writing.

LAN COMPONENTS

A number of elements must be considered when setting up a local area network, including the following basic components:

- Network server.
- Interface card.
- Network software.
- Application software.
- Cables.
- Training.

• Administration.

The **network server** is a computer whose basic role is to link shared peripheral devices and store commonly used information, such as customer account records, mailing lists, and inventory. Because the server is responsible for storing all information used on the network, it usually requires more than one hard drive with extensive storage capacity and powerful processing capabilities to handle all the requests for information it constantly receives.

Basically, two types of servers are used in a local area network: dedicated and non-dedicated. A dedicated server can act only as the server for the other microcomputers on the LAN. Because that server has been assigned a single task, it cannot perform any other function. A non-dedicated server, however, can act as a separate workstation in addition to serving the other microcomputers. A non-dedicated server tends to perform slowly because its tasks must be divided between serving the network and serving the person who is using it as a workstation. If the server is used as a workstation instead of being completely dedicated to the tasks necessary to maintain the network, the possibility of network failure increases. Any problems caused here can bring down the entire network.

Each computer within the local area network will require an **interface card** – the hardware that allows the machine to be connected to the server. Interface cards are small electronic boards that are inserted directly into the computer. Once they are installed, their presence and functioning are essentially invisible to the user. They operate like bridges that link otherwise isolated islands of equipment. There are a variety of cards to choose from, some offering faster access time to the central server than others.

Users have many options when choosing an interface cabling system. The three most popular are ARCnet, Ethernet, and Token Ring. ARCnet is the oldest, and also the slowest. Ethernet is usually in the middle, and Token Ring has the capacity to exceed all others in speed. (Of course, other factors affect the speed of the LAN besides the interface options.) Each option allows users to access information in different ways. Ask your vendor or consultant to suggest the option that's most appropriate for your information processing needs.

The **network software** performs all the functions necessary to administer the network workstations, storage devices, printers, and communications devices. The software is part of the network server, and it controls the shared devices, while DOS (or another type of operating system) is part of the workstation where it controls the local devices. Essentially, network software extends the computer's operating system to each workstation on the network. A small software program known as a shell links DOS to the network operating system. The shell interprets each command initiated by the user and sends requests to the appropriate destination – either the server or the workstation. The software co-ordinates the activities of the various network users by providing such things as simultaneous file updating by more than one user, password protection so that only those who are authorized can update files, printer support to manage the files sent by users, and so on. The selection of the appropriate network software is one of the more critical decisions involved in purchasing a network. Again, a major consideration is the application software you have selected for your company's needs. Since many software packages, accounting systems included, will operate only with certain LAN software programs, be sure to discuss your needs with your vendor or other experts to select the package that's right for your needs.

While most **application software** that runs on a standalone computer will also run on a local area network, LAN versions of the same software come with collision prevention routines, which standalone packages lack. These routines are built into the software to prevent errors resulting from more than one person at a time attempting access. Without these routines, the software can corrupt data.

The **cabling** used to connect each workstation can be a major cost in the implementation of your LAN. Generally, cable costs include the cable itself, the terminal connectors, and the labour necessary for an electrician to install the wiring. Costs can be trimmed by installing the cabling yourself. However, although relatively straightforward, cabling has to be done correctly. If not, intermittent signal problems could crop up. For example, if you lay a cable over a fluorescent light, you won't have a successful connection. Depending on the design of your building, the local building codes, and the distances between workstations, the cost per workstation can range significantly. Most offices are subject to a building code that governs how wiring can be distributed to the walls of the building. In some offices, for example, cable cannot simply be laid through the false ceiling and dropped through walls to connect offices.

Learning to manage the LAN is a difficult undertaking similar to learning a new operating system. The most effective approach is to nominate one staff member to act as the LAN administrator and have that individual obtain the technical training. Generally, **training** for a local area network is more expensive than conventional training because the instructor must have a high level of expertise and the equipment requirements are much greater. Other users of the system can then take less sophisticated courses or be taught by the LAN administrator.

Part of the duties of the LAN **administrator** will be to provide ongoing network support if anything goes wrong – if, for example, users cannot access the network from their workstations or if the printers stop working. If the network is properly installed, the LAN administrator's duties should not require much more than several hours per week. However, it is important to consider the time element when selecting the LAN administrator. Although the position is mainly clerical, the LAN administrator should also be prepared to help users understand how the network works, create passwords so new users can access the network, and make sure back-up copies are made.

LANS – DESIGN CONSIDERATIONS

There are many technical considerations involved in the design of a local area network. Normally, you would rely on an expert for recommendations in this area. The following are two important areas to be considered:

- Cabling type.
- Topology.

Cabling type refers to the kind of cables connecting each computer in the local area network. The four commonly used cables are:

- Twisted-pair.
- Coaxial cable.
- Fibre optic cable.

Twisted-pair cable is similar to the wire used in your telephone system. It is the simplest medium and generally the least expensive. In some cases, you may even be able to use the existing telephone wires in your building.

Shielded twisted-pair cable is similar to twisted pair cable except that it is protected from interference (from other cables, electrical devices, fluorescent lights) by a metallic shield. It is more expensive than regular twisted-pair, but provides higher reliability and performance.

Coaxial cable is a thicker cable, similar to the wire used to provide cable television to your home. Because of the thickness and the extra insulation used, coaxial is less subject to electrical interference than twisted-pair.

Fibre optic cable is a very thin glass strand along which laser light transfers data. Of the three, this cable represents the newest technology and can carry the most information. Fibre optic cable is particularly appropriate in areas that experience high electrical interference and in networks where the workstations are separated by great distances.

When choosing cable for your network, cost is just one of the considerations. In some cases, better-quality cable will result in less network downtime, allowing the cable to pay for itself.

The term **topology** describes the way computers are connected in a local area network. It's important to understand that only one workstation can access the server at the same time. That's why speed is such an important issue. The faster the server, the more information that can be processed throughout the network. A topology is the way in which requests for access to the server are managed. These are five common topologies, or patterns, and each assigns priority in a different way:

- Bus.
- Star.
- Tree.
- Ring or loop.
- Hybrid.

The **bus** topology follows a linear path and "stops" at each workstation along the way like a bus that picks up a passenger. All workstations are connected to a central cable that runs from one end of the LAN to the other. At each stop, the workstation is authorized to, in effect, board the bus so information from the workstation can be processed. If the workstation does not require access to the central server, the bus moves to the next stop.

The **star** topology connects each computer in the LAN to a wiring hub, which is usually placed in the centre of the network. The workstations and server are arranged in a circle around the hub in such a way that each computer represents a point in the star.

The **tree** topology is really a combination of a bus topology and a star topology. In the tree topology, the computers are like the leaves of a tree. They're connected to one another by a system of cables that branch through splitting devices to reach each other from the central server, which is essentially the root of the system. A **ring** or **loop** topology connects the computers in a ring to complete a closed circle. Because only one workstation is connected directly to the network, the remaining stations are completely dependent on one another. If one link in the chain is defective, none of the other workstations can function, causing the entire network to collapse.

The **hybrid** topology represents a combination of the star and ring layouts. The advantage of this system is that if one workstation fails, the others can continue to operate. The type of interface card and operating system you choose will usually dictate the kind of topology you use; still, always discuss your choices first with a qualified vendor or consultant. Local area networks are one area of technology you won't want to face alone.

5/The Importance of Training

Training is as important to the successful implementation of your computer system as the equipment you buy to help run your business. In fact, your company may have the best software on the market and the most powerful computer available, but unless you and your staff know how to use the system productively, you might just as well throw your investment away. Not training your staff to operate the computer is like hiring someone to do your books who knows nothing about accounting. By training your staff in the proper manner, you'll not only take advantage of your computer investment, you'll also:

- Save time that would have been spent learning by trial and error.
- Avoid costly errors.
- Learn to use the computer system (both hardware and software) to its fullest.
- Build staff confidence and morale.
- Help your staff avoid bad habits.
- Help your staff develop an understanding of how the system works.

Reduce Learning Time

When it comes to computer training, every day spent in the classroom can equal up to five days of on-the-job self-training, depending on the application involved. (Word processing, for example, would probably require significantly less self-training than general ledger.) That's five days during which the worker does little more than investigate the new system and try to absorb information that may or may not prove useful to your business. By not having the employee available for work, you not only lose the salary, you also lose the profit that employee is responsible for generating. As discussed later in this chapter, time is a major cost factor in the implementation of a computer, and any reduction in that time is a benefit to your business. Good-quality, properly focused training should save you money, not cost you money.

Marshall Electronics, a small manufacturing firm with 28 employees, recently purchased a computerized accounting system. The accounting manager, who earns about $25 dollars an hour (not counting overhead), was given the task of automating the general ledger. All responsibility for training was left to her. She had the choice of training herself or enroling in two classroom courses: Introduction to Computers, and General Ledger. She chose to train herself. After five days, she had learned enough about the computer and its operating system to feel comfortable. This same information could have been taught to her in one day by an experienced instructor. The general ledger system took even longer to learn. After ten days of trial and error, she gained a working knowledge, a level she could have reached in two days through classroom instruction. Furthermore, because there were large gaps in her understanding of the general ledger system, when her training phase was complete, she required technical support, at approximately $100 an hour, from an outside expert. In all, she spent 15 days learning the system and hundreds of dollars in support because she wanted to avoid the cost of professional instruction. The following chart shows how much she spent training herself compared to how much classroom instruction would have cost.

	Self-Taught		Classroom Training	
	Time	Expenses	Time	Expenses
Introduction to PC's and DOS	5 days (35 hrs.) @ $25 hr. = $875	Nil	1 day (7 hrs.) @ $25/ hr. = $175	$250 training fee
Introduction to General Ledger	10 days (70 hrs.) @ $25/ hr. = $1,750	Nil	2 days (14 hrs.) @ $25/ hr. = $350	$500 training fee
Post-Learning Support	5 hrs. @ $24/hr. = $125	5 hrs @ $100/hr. = $500	1 hr. @ $25/hr. = $25	1 hr. @ $100/hr. = $100
Total		$3,250		$1,400

As the table demonstrates, the accountant could have saved her company $1,850 by enroling in the training classes.

Avoid Costly Errors

In a computerized setting, information is your most vital resource. If you have an inventory system, all that information will be stored on the computer. In an accounting system, all up-to-date financial records are stored on the computer's hard drive. As well, most customer accounts are kept in a database. Losing that information can be disastrous. One of the biggest worries owner-managers have is the fear of losing accounts receivable data. Without a record of who owes your organization money, you have no way of collecting payment from your customers. It's vital that your staff be properly trained to protect important data such as this from deletion or corruption.

Many owner-managers don't realize that one of the biggest causes of computer error in most small businesses is the lack of training on the part of the operator. An untrained employee can accidentally wipe out an entire hard drive by trying to format a diskette (a simple procedure that requires minimal understanding of DOS commands). That's exactly what happened to Lakehead Press, a small publishing house that produced a quarterly catalogue for a large medical supply company. Although the company produced other publications, the catalogue was the most lucrative. It was also the largest, with about 600 pages including photographs. All product information was stored on a database. Because the information had to be constantly updated, only hard copy back-ups were maintained.

One day, a new employee needed to print a file from the database. To do so, he first had to copy the data onto a floppy diskette. The only diskettes available were brand new. They hadn't yet been formatted with the necessary information from the computer's operating system. The new employee thought he knew how to format a disk properly. But instead of carrying out this simple procedure, he accidentally formatted the computer's hard drive, wiping out the entire database used to produce the publication. That quarter, the catalogue was a little late.

Many costly errors such as this can be prevented with proper operator training. For example, many new computer users who haven't received introductory training in the use of software will panic when the program doesn't behave as expected. Perhaps a document won't print because the right printer isn't selected.

Perhaps the user accidentally asked the program to perform a function, then didn't know how to turn the function off, even though it requires only a few keystrokes to correct. In such a situation, many untrained users turn off the computer as a solution to the problem, not realizing that this can corrupt the data on diskette and damage the software program.

As an owner-manager, you must evaluate your risk areas and ensure that, at a bare minimum, training is received in the areas that could cause the most problems.

When assessing the training needs of your business, maintain a balance between the costs and the projected savings. You must balance the costs and the expected benefits to your firm and to your employees. Since it's unlikely you'll have an unlimited budget for training, remember to review the training plan for your staff and ensure that this plan focuses on the most important issues first.

Use System to Its Fullest

Modern microcomputer hardware and software is extremely powerful. However, most owner-managed businesses use only a small portion of the functions and capabilities available within the system, missing some of the benefits of automation. One of the main reasons for this inefficient use is a failure to train staff in all the functions and capabilities of the system. For example, your staff may be trained to generate a number of financial reports each month using your accounts receivable system. The task of generating these reports involves a lot of repetitive keystrokes. Most software of this kind comes with a function that allows the user to "save" all repetitive keystrokes and, by simply touching a key, play back each stroke exactly as recorded. Known as a macro function, this kind of operation usually requires a sound knowledge of the software program. Through proper training, users can be shown how to apply such time-saving features built into the software.

Many owner-managers use a computer to replace a manual system, not realizing that they can speed up and add functions. For example, under a manual system, you produce financial statements. A computer system can take the data used in the financial statements and create other reports, such as sales projections, and cost and profit-margin analyses.

Build Confidence and Morale

Just how adversely poor morale can affect your business is difficult to measure. But common sense suggests that employees who have confidence in what they are doing and who feel good about working for the organization are more productive than unhappy workers. Anything that threatens the morale of your staff must be handled delicately.

Introducing a computer system that alters the way work is performed can be an extremely demoralizing event, especially if employees are not properly trained to use the new equipment. In the end, your company's profits can be adversely affected. If your employees are continuously unsure of what is happening with their computers, they will feel a certain amount of negative stress. Training will build your staff's confidence and therefore improve morale. Your employees will be more confident in the work they do and in the results they obtain.

A small marketing research company that was going through a difficult time recently used training as a way to instil confidence in its employees. The company produces a series of market reports that it sells to a small group of clients. The reports contain forecast information and time-sensitive data. If a monthly report fails to get out on time, the information is useless to the clients. For years, the company relied on outside printing and typesetting. The process was expensive, and there was even talk of eliminating the entire service, just to save money. Instead, the company decided to purchase a desktop publishing system, which would eliminate at least one of the steps in the production process and help get material out the door in less time and for less money. At first, the staff who produced the material were nervous about the new system. They'd never worked on a computer before and didn't understand how it could save time and money. Furthermore, they were convinced that this step was a prelude to an eventual layoff – that the company would use their inability to produce the material in time as an excuse to eliminate the service and their jobs.

At this point, the owner-manager stepped in to explain the situation. He said the company realized things would be difficult in the beginning while everyone got used to the new system. But the company was prepared to wait. To help them learn desktop publishing, each employee was sent on an intensive training course. They learned how desktop publishing worked and how to apply it to their publications. Training demystified the process for them and convinced them that the company's plan was more than feasible. They quickly stopped worrying about being laid off because they had confidence in their ability to help the company reach its goals. The result was more timely information going out the door, which improved the company's reputation in the marketplace. And because the staff were under less pressure than before to meet deadlines, they had the time to experiment with different layouts and design, resulting in eye-catching documents that drew praise from a number of clients.

Avoid Learning Bad Habits

"The only way to learn to use a computer is to sit down and teach yourself." Everyone who has thought about computerizing has probably heard this sentiment expressed at one time or another. The downside is that the statement is partially true: you *can* learn to use a computer by trial and error. Of course, there's also a strong possibility that you will develop bad habits, such as failing to follow short cuts, not saving material when you should, and designing documents inefficiently.

Some people can learn to use software without assistance, especially applications that encourage creativity and experimentation, such as word processing and desktop publishing, where the quality of the product is subjective. The majority of us, however, need help to avoid teaching ourselves bad habits. In fact, learning through trial and error can sometimes be a dangerous method. Although many excellent books are available to help users learn software, the books are so general in nature than most people don't bother reading them cover to cover. If the user fails to read an important section because it didn't seem relevant at first, he or she ends up with only partial knowledge. You wouldn't want an employee who's read six chapters in a twelve-chapter book on spreadsheets to take over your company's budgeting.

Develop an Understanding

It's easier to do well at most jobs when you have a thorough understanding of what's required. Many people learn to work with computers by memorizing the procedures and not really understanding the process. The difference between understanding how something works and simply memorizing the mechanical procedures involved is what separates workers who can apply the methods independently in a variety of situations from those who require constant supervision. For example, an employee can be taught that pressing certain keys in a specific sequence causes a particular report to print. When a slightly different report is required, he'll have to be shown a different sequence of keys to press. People can be trained to understand the task, or they can be asked simply to memorize keystrokes. If your employees learn why those keys cause the report to be generated, they'll be much more likely to determine for themselves how to produce other reports on the system.

TRAINING PROCEDURES

When determining what training is required, three areas should be addressed:

- Computer training.
- Application training.
- Business (accounting) training.

Computer Training

Computer training teaches people to operate the computer itself and to understand the operating system and the basic commands and utilities required to work in a business environment. A general understanding of the basic functions of the computer hardware and how they interrelate is also taught to ensure that the equipment is used as efficiently as possible and to reduce the risk of costly errors. Understanding the basics involves knowing the commands built into the operating system. Your staff should be capable of making the simple commands that start a program, copy files, create back-up documents, and erase data. Such commands, like the diskette formatting procedure mentioned earlier, have a distinct language and syntax that must be closely followed. Any deviation could result in unexpected errors.

The amount of computer training your staff requires depends on the complexity of the system they're being asked to learn, their aptitude, and the type of hardware and software you're using. If your business is using a local area network, your staff may require additional training to become familiar with the different procedures related to sharing data, logging on to the network, and the numerous other matters of protocol that require emphasis in a network environment.

The *aptitude* of your staff is a major factor affecting the amount of computer training required. Some people seem much more capable of understanding the computer environment than others. Luckily, most people now entering the work force have been exposed to computers in high school and university. And as software becomes more user-friendly, even people with little or no computer experience can learn enough basic material to become productive in a short time.

To establish what level of computer training is required, each member of your staff should have an individual training plan. Talk to your staff to determine each person's level of knowledge based on experience and exposure to computers through school or previous employment. Most people have little experience and fit into the "new user" category. They require basic training, beginning with an introduction to PCs and your computer operating system.

The *type of hardware* you use in your business will also affect the amount of training required. Typically, the Apple Macintosh environment requires less computer training than a DOS-based environment, which in turn could require less instruction than the Unix operating system.

If your employees work independently at standalone workstations, they may have to master the technique of installing programs on the hard drive, using the floppy disk drives to switch from one data or program disk to another, and so on. In a local area network environment, the software programs your staff is likely to work with are probably already installed on the server. It is unlikely that the individual employee will ever have to master the intricacies of program installation. In such a case, you'd be advised to concentrate training in the area of application software. If you use Macintosh computers in your business, it's essential that your staff learn to operate a mouse as well as a keyboard. If your system is DOS- or Unix-based, you may not need to introduce the mouse, depending on the application software you're using. In any case, the type of hardware you use has implications for the kind of training your employees require, the duration of the courses, and the techniques and tools your staff should be expected to know.

Application Training

Application training involves teaching people to use specific software packages (general ledger, accounts receivable, accounts payable, word processing, spreadsheets, etc.). Because it deals directly with the software your staff will use to run your business, application instruction is the most important ingredient in the overall training package. The amount of training required depends on the complexity of the application and the experience of the student. If the student has previously worked with accounting and business software, a day of instruction may be all that's required. But if the person has never worked with this kind of software, more intensive training will likely be needed. To make sure your workers learn to use the many features available in the software, it's important to determine each person's level of competence and experience and to assign the training accordingly. Normally, your staff's application training requirements will not be affected by the hardware environment (i.e., Apple Macintosh versus DOS). Training should be based on your staff's skills.

Business (Accounting) Training

The successful implementation of a computer system in a small business requires a sound understanding of business and accounting. For instance, one of the most common applications of a spreadsheet program in an owner-managed business involves the development of business plans, cash flows, and projections. Successful application of this type of software requires not only knowledge of the program but a good understanding of business as well.

Just as learning to use a word processor will not make you a good writer, learning to use an accounting software package will not make you a good accountant. In order to use an accounting application properly in your business, your staff must understand basic accounting. It's all right, for example, to misspell a word in word processing software (most programs have a spell-check feature that will catch many errors), but if you incorrectly post a journal entry to a general ledger, the mistake may be harder to detect.

In most cases, it's easier to teach basic computer skills to someone with an accounting background than it is to teach accounting skills to someone with a computer background. You should therefore take your staff's business skills into consideration when designing a training plan. Perhaps you need to enrol some of your workers in bookkeeping courses as well as computer training.

REVIEW STAFF CAPABILITIES

It is important to develop a training plan that is appropriate to your organization and your staff. Start by reviewing the qualifications and capabilities of your staff and matching those with job descriptions and the tasks that must be learned. Let's say an employee has no prior computer experience. Extensive training might seem to be a logical requirement. However, after analyzing the person's job description, you discover the majority of her work is performed in areas unrelated to computers. Clearly, she won't require the same level of training as someone who operates a computer every day.

Your training plan could take several forms. In the following three-step example, we start by documenting the staff's existing level of knowledge in areas of particular importance to the organization. The following "Skills Matrix" helps us rank the staff's level of expertise. Next, we create a similar matrix, only this time we substitute the rank we want the staff to achieve.

PRESENT UNDERSTANDING OF SOFTWARE APPLICATION
on a scale of 1 to 5

	DOS	General Ledger	Spreadsheet	Database	Word Pro.
Accounting Manager (Laurel)	2	2	0	0	3
Budget Manager (Kevin)	2	0	5	2	5
Office Trouble Shooter (Julie)	5	0	0	3	5
Marketing Manager (Ron)	2	0	2	5	2
Accounting Clerk (Sharon)	2	0	3	0	3

LEVEL OF UNDERSTANDING NECESSARY

	DOS	General Ledger	Spreadsheet	Database	Word Pro.
Laurel	2	**5**	**2**	0	3
Kevin	2	0	5	**5**	**2**
Julie	5	0	**2**	3	5
Ron	2	0	**5**	5	**4**
Sharon	**5**	**3**	3	0	3

(Highlighted figures indicate changes to the previous chart.)

The owner-manager wants Laurel to be proficient with the general ledger software and Sharon to train as Laurel's back-up. The owner wants everyone to have a good understanding of DOS, with one "expert" (Julie) and a back up (Sharon). The second identifies which employees require training and exactly how much instruction they require. The third step is to develop a training plan for each person.

Training Requirements

Training Programs	Laurel	Kevin	Julie	Ron	Sharon
Introduction to Micros					X
General Ledger	X				X
Spreadsheets	X		X	X	
Database Management		X			
Word Processing				X	

TYPE OF TRAINING AVAILABLE

Computer training is available in a variety of formats, ranging from traditional classroom methods of instruction to systems that make use of the latest technological advances in interactive self-study, but there are basically four techniques:

- Classroom training.
- One-on-one training.
- Video training.
- Computer-aided instruction.

Classroom Training

Classroom training is the most traditional method of computer instruction available. In most classroom situations, a single instructor passes information along to a group of participants. Course material is usually pre-determined and relatively rigid, although instructors can alter the focus depending on the needs of the group. In a classroom environment, your employees will have an opportunity to interact with people who have similar problems. Such interactions can often enhance the training experience.

However, classroom training has disadvantages. For one thing, the success of the course usually depends on the instructor's attitude, skills, and enthusiasm. Another disadvantage is that most courses are offered at set times, which may not coincide with your training needs. Classroom training also takes place for the most part in locations outside the work site. If a key member of your staff is away on training when an emergency arises, you may run into difficulty.

Also, as long as your staff is away from work, that time counts as lost productivity, which should be figured into the overall training costs.

One-on-One Training
As the name implies, one-on-one training is more interactive than classroom instruction. In most cases, it's also more flexible, allowing for input and feedback from the student. Although one-on-one instruction typically involves one instructor and one student, the format can be expanded to include a small group of participants. The biggest advantage of this type of training is the customized service that is provided. Instruction focuses on the student's greatest weaknesses. The lesson advances only when the student is ready. As well, instructors can deal with the day-to-day problems of the business, providing the student with practical knowledge that can be applied directly to the job. Overall, compared to other systems of training, one-on-one instruction is very time efficient because no extraneous material is introduced. It can also provide the students with instant feedback and quick answers to their questions. Since one-on-one training is usually user-defined and interactive, your organization gets what it wants and only what it wants. Like classroom instruction, however, this training method depends on the instructor's skills. One-on-one training is usually provided on an hourly basis and can be very expensive.

Video Training
With VCRs and other video technology becoming more commonplace, video training is quickly emerging as a popular alternative to more conventional methods of instruction. With video training, the user is taken step-by-step through a programmed tutorial. The participant watches a step on the video tape, then performs the step on the computer.

Video training can be very cost effective because your organization can rent the videos at a reasonably low costs. Video training can reduce scheduling problems because the video can be viewed at the convenience of your staff. However, the technology is still somewhat new, and many people experience mixed results using video.

Video training is particularly good for teaching concepts and generic topics such as an introduction to computers and DOS. Your organization could probably use video training for a portion of the computer training program. Since it's designed to reach a wide audience, video training is generic in nature. As such, it is not usually applicable for business training or application training, nor is it very useful for the specific requirements of your organization. Another complaint often heard about video training is that there is no feedback mechanism to determine what the participants have learned.

Computer-Aided Instruction

In computer-aided instruction programs, the computer itself teaches a specific topic. These programs present the participants with information, then test, using online simulations and practice sessions, to determine how well the material has been understood. Based on the test results, either a review of old material or a lesson covering new ground is initiated. Computer-aided instruction is a powerful teaching tool. It's quite useful for teaching generic topics, such as keyboard and typing skills, and basic operating knowledge. However, the cost of developing computer-aided instructions that meet the specific needs of owner-managed businesses is generally quite high. Computer-aided instruction is not readily available to most owner-managed businesses except for generic training.

LOOK FOR THE BEST COMBINATION

There is no one computer training solution that is right for all businesses. After reviewing the needs of your organization, you must decide on the best combination of the various training methods for you. Usually, classroom and one-on-one training are the most cost-effective alternatives for owner-managed businesses. Video is good for the basic concepts, while computer-aided instruction is very good for the limited subjects it covers. Depending on the number of people being trained, however, you may want to consider purchasing a video or a computer-aided system rather than relying on instructors. These methods have the advantage of a set cost, regardless of the number of students. In most cases, a combination of techniques proves to be the most efficient to train employees. Be sure to consider all your alternatives before making a decision.

SELECTING APPROPRIATE CLASSROOM TRAINING

In spite of the variety of training methods available, most owner-managed businesses rely on classroom instruction for their staff. The following section provides a breakdown of the components that go into a sound classroom-based program. Use this breakdown as a guide when selecting the appropriate course for your staff.

DEFINE OBJECTIVES

The first thing to consider before deciding on a program is what each staff member needs to learn. The training requirements (computer, application, or business) and the level of competence required to carry out the demands of the business will greatly affect the selection of a training vendor. At this point, you should define your staff capabilities. (See earlier "Review Staff Capabilities" section.)

WHERE TO GO FOR TRAINING

Most owner-managed businesses are constantly bombarded with training brochures. Typical sources for training include universities and community colleges, computer vendors, accounting firms, and independent training organizations. It's important to match your training requirements with the program best suited to your needs. Asking for additional information and requesting references can help you decide what route to take.

HANDS-ON VERSUS LECTURE

When it comes to classroom computer training, two methods are most common: hands-on training and instruction by lecture. Hands-on training gives participants access to computers and allows them to work on the techniques presented in the seminar. In a lecture format, computers are not available and the focus is on concepts and techniques. Hands-on training is usually most appropriate for computer and application training, because it allows students to work directly with the software and equipment in a situation similar to the workplace and to encounter and solve everyday problems in a controlled environment. Lecture-style training is usually most appropriate for accounting and business training. However, the most effective method for accounting software training is to combine a lecture approach with hands-on instruction, since students are taught the basic concepts of automated accounting and are then able to apply their new knowledge.

TRAINING FACILITY

When selecting a training vendor, look at the quality of the training facility. You should consider:

- Type of equipment.
- Type of software.
- Operating system used.

- Student-to-computer ratio.
- Presentation equipment.
- General facilities.

The **computer equipment** should be similar to the equipment used in your organization. For example, if your organization is primarily using Apple Macintoshes, training on IBM or IBM compatible computers will not be beneficial; in fact, it might prove quite the opposite. Problems can also be caused with different keyboards. If your organization consistently uses one type of keyboard, it may be appropriate to look for a training facility that uses a similar keyboard. Some training vendors use laptop computers to instruct students, even though keyboard arrangement can be noticeably different from most desktop layouts. This difference can lead to confusion in the classroom and back at the office.

The **software** used during training should be the same as the package used by your organization. Although many of the concepts are similar from one program to another, using different programs can result in confusion and errors on the job. Even new releases of the same product can differ enough to require separate training. For example, if a word processing program that uses function keys extensively to access menus and commands revised the set-up of the system, users would have to learn the new orientation. A popular word processing program for the DOS environment once altered its package to allow for the integration of text and graphics. The features were so new to the program, and so powerful, that most experienced users required training to take advantage of all the package had to offer.

Of course, there are extreme examples. Some software developers tend to be much more consistent with their user interface (the way the operator works with the software) than others. Individuals using one of the more popular spreadsheets on the market benefit from this consistency. Each release of the product follows the same interface, greatly reducing learning time.

The type of training previously received by the user will affect the length of time it takes to become familiar with the updated package. Some instructors tend to teach the students specific keystrokes related to specific functions. Good instructors spend more time teaching the concepts so the user understands the process instead of just the keystrokes to follow. A student who understands the concepts will be in a better position to transfer the knowledge from one version to the next – even when different applications are involved.

The user's level of sophistication also affects the training needed when new versions of a program are released. Most users use only the very basic functions available within a package. These basic functions rarely change as software is updated, so these users require little training. On the other hand, users who continually stretch the software to its limits often find new techniques and approaches available in new releases. Training helps them learn the new procedures quickly and efficiently.

Make certain the **operating system** is consistent with the one being used in your business. For example, it would be very difficult to learn to use Unix – or the Apple Macintosh, for that matter – on computers operating in a DOS-based environment. The reverse also applies.

Depending on the type of training required, the **student-to-computer ratio** will vary. Instruction on how to use the computer and its operating system, for instance, often requires a computer for every student. For most business-related application training, a two-to-one ratio represents the optimum arrangement for a number of reasons. For one thing, classes tend to move at the speed of the slowest participant. By properly matching participants in teams of two, the entire class can cover more material and learn more effectively. As well, individuals tend to learn by their mistakes. By working in groups of two, they can learn from each other. Finally, participants typically have more confidence when working in teams. They are more willing to experiment and will often learn more than if left on their own.

Your staff will learn much more if the training is presented using appropriate **presentation equipment**. The computer training centre should be equipped with appropriate audio-visual tools, such as sound, slides, an overhead projector, a white board and a flip chart. A computer projection screen is an effective method for speeding up the learning process. This equipment allows the instructor to project an image of the computer screen that the entire group can see. As a result, participants can follow each step and watch the operations be carried out.

Finally, the **facilities** should be comfortable and well equipped with large tables and good chairs. Appropriate lighting is especially important when audio-visual equipment is being used. If you're discussing a significant amount of training for your staff, you may want to request a tour of the training facility to ensure that it meets your standards.

INSTRUCTOR

As mentioned, classroom training depends on the quality of the instruction and the skills and credentials of the instructor. Many organizations use part-time instructors for their training. These people may have little or no qualifications to teach computer classes. For training involving accounting software, the instructor should have the appropriate business qualifications. If a large amount of training is being purchased, you may want to ask for and check the references of the instructors.

When selecting a training vendor, ask what the maximum student-to-instructor ratio will be. For most business-related applications, the optimum student/instructor ratio is approximately 10 to one, with a maximum of 12 to one.

COURSEWARE

Courseware is a term used to describe the design of the course and the participant manuals. The course should be designed in a modular format that presents participants with small chunks of information and gives them an opportunity to understand that information before they move on. Each module should have clear objectives and exercises to test and provide feedback to the participants.

Participant manuals should be clear, concise, and easy to understand. Not only should they serve as manuals during the presentation of the course, they should also provide an ongoing reference source for participants after the training is over. The best participant manuals present information while leaving room for participants to incorporate their own notes and information provided by the instructor. When selecting a training vendor, you may want to review the participant manuals to ensure that the courseware meets the needs of your organization.

STAFF CONSIDERATIONS

Training is an investment, and a trained employee is a valuable resource to your organization. As an employer, you may want to protect your investment by entering into a contract with your employee for all matters relating to training. Some organizations, for example, encourage their employees to enrol in job-related training by agreeing to reimburse the cost of the instruction if the employee remains with the company for a certain time following successful completion of the course. Others pay for employee training up front but treat the expense as an interest-free loan, which is considered paid in full only when the worker has stayed with the organization for a specified time. If the employee leaves before this, the training "loan" must be repaid. Although this arrangement may not be practical for your organization, an employment contract or similar agreement may help you protect your training investment. These days, trained computer operators are in constant demand, and qualified workers often have their pick of jobs. To reduce the risk of losing employees once you've made a major investment in their training, some kind of policy should be considered.

6 / Converting to a Computerized System

Conversion is the process of transferring data from your existing system to the new computerized system. With some applications, such as word processing, this procedure can be very straightforward. In fact, for the most part, the process requires simply that form letters, addresses, and other standard documents be made available electronically. In other applications, such as accounting systems, conversion can be extremely complex, often requiring careful advance planning.

As a central Ontario printing house found out, being unprepared can lead to lengthy delays in getting the new system running. Originally, the printing house invested about $12,000 in computer hardware and accounting software. During the first eight months, the staff received some training, but not enough to feel confident about abandoning the old system for the new one. As a result, the computer remained inoperational.

After interviewing each of his employees, the owner-manager realized that part of the problem was that his staff felt overwhelmed by all the components of the new system. He therefore developed a plan to ease the strain of conversion. Instead of doing it all at once, he worked out a logical order that introduced the computer system one component at a time, and a schedule that allowed time for staff to learn each component before moving on to the next. As a result, conversion proceeded smoothly and efficiently. By assigning specific tasks to each staff member and assigning deadlines for completion, the owner-manager was able to get the new system fully operational within three months. Without proper planning, the time would have been wasted.

DEVELOP A PLAN

Once you have decided to automate your accounting system, it is tempting to convert all systems at once so your business can start saving money. Such an attitude will result only in disappointment. It is difficult enough to convert one segment of the accounting system. Any more than that and you run the risk of making errors from which your business will have a hard time recovering. If your business is converting to a computer system for the first time, your conversion plan should guide you through each stage of the process. It should identify which applications should be converted first, the amount of time needed for the conversion, and the appropriate deadlines to be met. When developing your conversion plan, the following two rules should be observed:

- Convert each application in its logical order.
- Allow time between the conversion of applications.

Logical Order

Your computerization plan is only as sound as the thought you put into it. The more logical the steps you follow are, the greater the chance that your plan will succeed. When developing a plan, be sure to include all applications to be converted. To determine a logical order in which to convert the applications, consider these functions:

- Payback.
- Logical progression.
- Business cycle.
- Fiscal year-end.
- Complexity.

The **payback** is the benefit you expect from a particular application. In Chapter 2 we discussed methods of determining the potential benefits of computerized accounting applications. When determining the most logical order of conversion for your business, first convert those applications that offer the largest payback. If you stand to gain more by converting an inventory system than an order entry package, you should consider starting with the former.

The conversion of most accounting systems also follows a **logical progression** based on how the various applications interact. For instance, in most distribution companies, the order entry and inventory control applications are the most critical. Inventory is particularly important, since it is the area in which most companies have the bulk of their money invested. Since order entry systems rely on information provided by inventory control – such as product number and description, quantity of stock on hand, and pricing – it's almost always necessary to convert the inventory control system before the order entry system. A similar relationship exists between retail invoicing packages and accounts receivable packages if customers charge purchases to their accounts. Linking the two systems allows a customer's balance to be updated following each purchase, reducing the risk of over-extending the credit limits. These two packages should therefore be converted together.

Your **business cycle** may also be a decisive factor. For instance, if your organization does a physical inventory count every six months, it would be beneficial to plan the conversion of inventory control around one of the planned inventory counts, thereby eliminating the need for an additional count at the conversion date. If business slows down at various times during the business cycle, or if inventory declines at particular times of the year, any one of these periods would be an ideal time to introduce an accounting software system. The reduced number of transactions or items and the additional time available to your staff will simplify the conversion process.

Your **fiscal year-end** is a good time to convert to the general ledger application software, since at this time your business normally has accurate opening balances. Without these, the information obtained from the system will never be correct. Typically, small businesses have their financial information reviewed by an accountant at year-end. This presents an excellent opportunity, since the year-end information supplied by the accountant can be used as the opening balance for the computer system. If your organization typically works on a cash basis, in which revenues are recorded when cash is received and expenses deducted when cheques are written, you may have accurate accounts payable and accounts receivable lists (called accruals) only at year-end. If you convert your accounts receivable and accounts payable at that time, revenue for the current year will be more accurately recorded. Since government reporting requires that payroll records accumulate to the calendar year-end, December 31 is an excellent time to convert a payroll system.

The **complexity** of the application may also determine the best time for conversion. In most cases, beginning with a simple application, such as inventory control (which involves a great deal of data entry, manual counting, and the inclusion of suppliers, alternative items, prices, etc.), the sheer volumes of work may prevent you from meeting your schedule. You may also be so discouraged by the process that you decide to postpone future applications. By starting with a simple software program, you and your staff will gain the experience and confidence to take on more challenging applications.

Allow Time Between Conversions

When scheduling the implementation of an accounting system, be sure to allow a break following each successful conversion to give your staff the opportunity to work out any problems in the procedures or in the accounting software. This time will also give them a chance to become comfortable with the new software, which will increase their confidence for the next stage in the process. Many software packages handle transaction-processing in a similar manner. For example, entering sales invoices in accounts receivable is much the same as entering supplier invoices in accounts payable. Once employees have become familiar with one application, they will be more capable of carrying out the next application, thus reducing the time spent training for the second application.

PRE-CONVERSION CONSIDERATIONS

Converting from a manual system to a computerized system is a lot like driving a car. Setting the car in motion is simple enough. But unless you check beforehand to make certain all systems are in working order – that there's enough gas in the car, and that steering, headlights, brakes, and horn are functioning – the outcome of your journey may be in doubt. Before converting any computerized application, a number of key factors must be taken into consideration:

- Ensure that hardware and software are operational.
- Ensure that staff have received appropriate training.
- Ensure that the previous accounting system is in order.
- Address other application-specific considerations.

Operational Hardware and Software

Long before you even consider converting your accounting requirements to an automated system, be sure that the hardware and software you have purchased are working properly. Your vendor should have installed the software on your computer's hard drive. Good-quality accounting software should come with a set of demonstration files and manuals that include exercises and tutorials to help you test the programs and familiarize yourself with how they work. Your vendor should have tested the hardware to make sure it's compatible with the software you've selected.

Your accounting system will also require various supplies, including paper, printer ribbons, and forms (cheques, invoices, statements). Be sure you have all these on hand for the conversion process.

Appropriate Training

As discussed in Chapter 5, proper training is essential if you expect your staff to operate the accounting software correctly. This training should include basic computer instruction, appropriate application-specific training, and the necessary business or accounting training. If your staff is not properly trained, you dramatically increase the risk that the conversion will fail.

Existing Accounting System in Order

Many owner-managers mistakenly believe that bringing a computer into their companies will automatically solve all their management problems. Unfortunately, computers cannot work miracles. If your existing accounting system is not in order, the best a computer can do is maintain the status quo. Make sure, therefore, that your existing system is balanced and under control before attempting to convert a computerized system. In particular, make sure your bank accounts have been reconciled and your general ledger control accounts agree with detailed records (accounts receivable, accounts payable, and inventory control).

Other Application-Specific Considerations

When including pre-conversion considerations in your plan, you should address each application separately. For just as different applications are more or less complex and more or less important to your business, each one also has special problems that must be addressed in advance. For example, **general ledger** conversions are most affected by the proposed financial reports required from this system. It's important to ensure that you have a good understanding of what financial reports are required to manage your business properly. Among the reports that you should consider are separate income statements for each branch, region, and province, which may in turn determine the numbering sequence you use in your chart of accounts. A chart of accounts is a list of accounts, often grouped by type. For instance, if you want to track telephone expenses and courier charges, you would set up two accounts. At the end of each period, total expenses are calculated, based on the transactions in these accounts.

Pre-conversion considerations for **accounts receivable** include a plan for obtaining the information to be entered into each customer's computer files, including credit limits, contacts, and sales tax exemption numbers. If you determine in advance what information is required, you reduce the likelihood of leaving out critical customer data. Your new monthly customer statements may also require new printed forms. Be sure you give your printing company enough time to produce your order. Ignoring these steps will increase the time it takes to get your new accounts receivable system running.

For **accounts payable** conversions, it's important to determine the design of the cheques and the accompanying forms that indicate which invoices the cheques have been issued for. You may have to print new cheques and forms. Leaving this to a late date could cause delays in getting the payables system started, resulting in extra work for your staff, since they'll be forced to continue to prepare cheques manually and to enter the information into the accounts payable system.

There are many pre-conversion considerations related to **inventory control**. The layout of the warehouse, the numbering system, the pricing policies, and vendor information must all be considered before the conversion.

When an inventory system is installed for the first time, the owner-manager often has to rearrange the warehouse to accommodate the new system. For example, it may be necessary to introduce an aisle and shelf locating system to make use of the software's ability to print this information on picking slips. Such a system makes it easier for the shippers to find stock, but you must consider the cost of not shipping any goods while the warehouse is being reorganized.

Product numbering systems may have to be restructured. You may wish to introduce a numbering system that provides information about the product itself (for example, style, colour, size, etc.) and that uses your own product number rather than that provided by suppliers. The decisions you make here are critical, since once the system is in place you can't change your method without re-entering all product information.

Printing policies should be considered before conversion takes place. In many automated packages, the order entry system uses pricing information obtained from inventory control. Once you adopt a policy in inventory control, it will be used by the order entry system.

Vendor information is another important area to consider. If you do business with a lot of vendors, or if a vendor uses a different product code for the same item, make sure you collect this information in advance and enter it into the system during the conversion. If you fail to include this information in the inventory package, you won't be able to utilize all the features available. For instance, when you reorder merchandise, it's important to know who sells that particular item. Unless this information is entered into the system, you can't be certain of identifying that particular supplier.

For **retail invoicing** systems, the design of the invoice and credit note forms should be developed before the conversion process to give your printer some lead time to obtain the design you want.

TAILORING THE SOFTWARE TO MEET YOUR ORGANIZATION'S NEEDS

Once you have developed a conversion plan, the next step is to adjust the software to your business. Most software now comes with built-in customization options that allow you to tailor the software to your needs. As part of your conversion plan, you should have examined these options carefully. Selecting the incorrect options may require you to reinstall a package the right way later on.

When tailoring or customizing the accounting software for your organization, follow this procedure:

- Understand the options available to you.
- Consider the effect of these options on the other applications in your plan.
- Select all options.
- Review workarounds.

Understand the Options

Sophisticated accounting software often comes with an overwhelmingly large range of options you can customize to your exact needs. It is important to understand each of these options and how they affect the software. For example, while most organizations require 12 accounting periods (one for each month), some companies work on a four-week accounting period, which means they require 13 periods per year. For these companies, the software that allows them to select the number of accounting periods is best.

Consider Effect on Other Applications

Be sure that you understand how the different options will affect the other applications you plan to install now and in the future. Many packages can operate independently of one another, but they also often contain options that activate information-sharing with other modules in the system. These options range from those that just look at information, such as general ledger account number, stored in another module's masterfile to those that actually transfer data like invoice information produced in an order entry to an accounts receivable file. If you don't examine your needs before deciding which modules should be linked together, you may have to reinstall the entire system to correct your oversight.

Select All Options First

Before installing your system, decide which options you require. Once you have gone through the options and made decisions for each one, tailoring your accounting software becomes a simple task. Organizations that make the mistake of waiting until they actually begin working with the software before selecting options usually end up making the wrong choices.

Review Workarounds

In Chapter 3 we discussed workarounds and how they affect the use of applications in your organization. It's important to review any planned workarounds while you're deciding on system options, since workarounds often affect the options you select for your organization. For example, a popular accounting package doesn't allow you to use accounts that track volume rather than dollars. If your company sells items according to volume – as a service station sells gasoline – you may need to keep track of the amount sold as well as the dollar value. A workaround designed for this program lets you set up an extra "dummy" account to store statistical information, such as the number of litres sold. Since dummy accounts aren't included in the financial statements, they have no effect on financial results.

Seek Help

In most accounting systems, the software-tailoring process is one of the more critical steps in the conversion process. If you are unsure of what options you require, get help from your computer vendor, your software publisher, or an independent consultant. Since people should have experience in working with the software in a wide range of organizations, they can help you select the right options for your organization.

NUMBERING SYSTEMS

The numbering system you choose is critical. This numbering system typically is included on the master files which are the standard information included within each application. All applications have master files. In an accounts receivable system, for instance, the master files contain information on all the company's customers. In an accounts payable system, the master files contain information about the vendors. Each item in these files has a unique identifier (for example, an account number in the chart of accounts, an item number in inventory control, and a customer number in accounts receivable). This item number can be used in many ways to sort and group information. For example, you may decide that all receivable customer accounts from 10000 to 19999 will represent customers located in Alberta, while 20000 to 29999 will be assigned to Newfoundland customers.

When numbering the information in your application, select a numbering system that allows you to insert additional records at a later date. You might, for instance, initially use only every tenth number.

GENERAL LEDGER – DESIGNING THE CHART OF ACCOUNTS

The most critical step in the implementation of a general ledger, that is, the proper design of the chart of accounts, starts with a review of management objectives and an analysis of which financial information will be required to meet these objectives. Once the financial statements have been designed, a chart of accounts should be developed to provide the information required to prepare this financial information.

When developing the chart of accounts for the general ledger system, you can greatly facilitate the formatting of financial reports at a later date by grouping similar accounts. For instance, a financial report may have a line for sales from four or five sales accounts. If these accounts are grouped together, it will be easier for the financial statement to gather this information from the chart of accounts.

Departmental reporting can be simplified by numbering the various departments in a logical way. Table 6.1 demonstrates such a system. In our example below, the organization has branches in six cities in four provinces across Canada. The organization is divided into a western region and an eastern region. Within the regions, each province was measured independently. The organization wanted to be able to obtain financial information at four levels:

- Entire country.
- By region.
- By province.
- By branch.

Table 6.1 Numbering System

Western Region			Eastern Region		
Alberta	Saskatchewan		Ontario		Quebec
Calgary	Saskatoon	Regina	Toronto	Hamilton	Montreal
1110	1210	1220	2110	2120	2210

By logically numbering each branch, the organization was able to obtain the required reports. All departments in the western region use a first digit of 1. All departments in the eastern region have a first digit of 2. The second digit relates to the province within a region. The Alberta branches have the first two digits of 11 and the Saskatchewan branches have the first two digits 12. Within each province, the branches are numbered sequentially in increments of 10. Using this numbering scheme, the organization was able to obtain financial reports using the following department ranges:

DEPARTMENTS INCLUDED	DEPARTMENT NUMBER RANGE
Canada wide	ALL
Western Region	1110-1220
Eastern Region	2110-2210
Alberta	1110
Saskatchewan	1210-1220
Ontario	2110-2120
Quebec	2210
Specific Branches	By Number

ACCOUNTS RECEIVABLE – CLIENT NUMBERING SYSTEMS

Depending on the accounts receivable software being used, customers can be grouped by region, by type, or by territory. Some less sophisticated software does not allow customers to be looked up by name. If yours doesn't, you may want to use several letters from the customer's name as part of the customer number to assist you in identifying customer numbers.

ACCOUNTS PAYABLE – VENDOR NUMBERING SYSTEM

Again, depending on the software you plan to introduce into your business, the vendor's identification number can be used to obtain additional information, including the types of products being purchased from these vendors. Also, the vendor number can be used to sort vendors by province and territory.

INVENTORY CONTROL – ITEM NUMBERING SYSTEMS

The item number is often used to group various types of inventory. A retail clothing store, for example, might use an item number that includes a colour code and size description, while a retail tire store might include tire size in its numbers. You might want to structure your item numbers to contain product information. The first two digits, for example, could represent the product category or line, the next four digits could be the model number, and so on. If in your business the majority of the products come from one supplier, you may decide to use the supplier's product numbers to avoid confusion – especially if the numbers appear on the product package. Employees can often mistake the number printed on the box for their own product code.

BACK-UP PROCEDURES

As mentioned in Chapter 4, all hard disks fail. It's just a question of when. Usually, "when" is the worst possible time. Getting caught without back-up copies can be devastating. Imagine, for example, losing all your customer information. Or all your accounts receivable data. That's why it's so important to implement back-up procedures from the very first day of the conversion process. The risk of not backing up your data is equal to the amount of time (and money) it would take to duplicate the information if you lost it all.

Backup procedures involve systematically storing information and records on some kind of storage system, such as diskette or tape drive, and using a log to document where this information is contained. How often you create back-ups should depend on the amount of risk involved if you lost that data. Critical information that would be very expensive to re-enter should be backed up much more frequently than information that is easily replaced and not critical to the organization.

Normally, only one person should be responsible for carrying out back-up procedures, and that person should receive the technical training needed to perform the duty.

Finally, a sound back-up program should include a method of documenting the current status of the back-ups. The documentation should indicate which tape or diskette holds the back-up information, the date that the back-up was completed, and the individual responsible. Table 6.2 is an example of a back-up log used by one of our clients.

Table 6.2 Back-up Log

Date	Program	Series	No. of Disks	Initial

CONVERSION CONTROLS

When converting from a manual to an automated accounting system, it is often hard to make sure that the opening numbers are complete and accurate. Without conversion control to ensure that all the information has been entered into the new system, there would be no procedure to verify the accuracy of the opening numbers. Generally, conversion controls vary according to application, although the basic principle is the same. Like an invoice that requires a manager's signature so it can be processed, conversion controls act as a kind of safety net.

To obtain complete and accurate opening balances, it is essential to have a clear cut-off point so all revenues and expenses related to a specific period can be "matched." For example, an organization could select the tenth of every month as its cut-off day. All invoices up until that day would belong to the previous month. As discussed previously, it may be advantageous to convert your accounting systems at strategic times during the year when a clear cut-off is being completed for other reasons. Year-end is an obvious example of a natural cut-off time.

GENERAL LEDGER

The best cut-off time for the general ledger is at the fiscal year-end. At this time, most organizations typically perform a detailed review that produces accurate financial information. However, in most cases, general ledger conversion can be carried out at any month-end if your organization is satisfied with the accuracy of the accounting information at that time. When converting to a new general ledger, check these key controls:

- Is the trial balance in balance (ie., do debits equal credits)?
- Do the total debits from the old system equal total debits on the new system?
- Is the opening balance sheet in balance?
- Does the general ledger agree with sub-ledgers such as accounts receivable and accounts payable?
- Is the chart of accounts conversion accurate?

The trial balance is a listing of all general ledger accounts and their current value. Ensuring that the **trial balance** is in balance is a basic control procedure that should be done before and after the conversion. Most sophisticated accounting software will not allow you to post an out-of-balance batch.

Making sure that **total debits** from the previous system equal the total debits from the new system will verify that all accounts have been completely entered. Most accounting software will provide you with total debits and total credits information from your trial balance.

To verify that the **opening balance sheet** is in balance, add all the balance sheet accounts or print the balance sheet to ensure that no profit-and-loss accounts have been mixed with the balance sheet accounts.

The system is not completely in balance until you **ensure the general ledger agrees with the sub-ledgers**. These include the bank reconciliation, reconciliation of accounts receivable and accounts payable control accounts, and in many cases reconciliations of other sub-ledgers such as fixed assets, inventory control, and payroll.

The **accurate conversion of a new chart of accounts** can be a problem when the account numbering system has changed. Review all information to ensure that it has all been converted accurately from the old numbering system to the new numbering system.

When converting general ledger systems, you must decide whether to input historical information from the prior year. Often, historical information is difficult and time-consuming to enter. For most owner-managed businesses it is better during the first year to obtain last year's history from manual information. In subsequent years the system will automatically update the historical information.

ACCOUNTS RECEIVABLE

Accounts receivable conversion can usually be completed at any month-end. It is important to document which invoices were posted to the system before the cut-off date and which after the cut-off date. This check will ensure that invoices are not entered into the system twice by mistake. When posting information to the new system, make sure that the opening balance (the account balances entered in the new system) is in agreement with the old system, both in total and by aging group. This will help to make sure that you have converted all the data from the old system correctly to the computerized system. Also confirm that the accounts receivable system agrees with the general ledger.

ACCOUNTS PAYABLE

Converting an accounts payable system at any month-end is a fairly simple undertaking. To help confirm that the conversion has been successful, total payables from the old system should be checked against total payables with the new system. Also, the accounts payable system must agree with the general ledger.

INVENTORY CONTROL

To ensure that the correct opening balances are entered into the inventory control system, a physical count is often necessary. By going to the warehouse and counting all items in stock, the total value of the inventory can be determined. Next, make sure that the general ledger agrees with the total determined by the physical count. Pay attention to receiving and shipping to make sure all items that have been received in the receiving area are included in inventory and all items that are considered shipped are not included in the count.

RUNNING PARALLEL

Running parallel means keeping the old system operational while running the new accounting system. This procedure involves a lot of duplicated effort, since all transactions and adjustments must be processed in both the old and new systems. The objective of running parallel is to make sure that the new system is running properly.

To determine whether you want to run parallel during the implementation and conversion of your organization's accounting systems, consider the risk of failure versus the cost of running two systems simultaneously. In most cases, running parallel systems for all the accounting functions is a luxury few organizations can afford.

When using pre-packaged software, the risk of problems developing with the new software is minimal, since most programs are thoroughly tested before they arrive at the vendor. The major concern is that the appropriate accounting procedures have been applied. Again, the risk is reduced if your procedures have been properly designed. Your risk will be further reduced if printed audit trails of all information entered in the system are available.

Look at your particular situation and decide accordingly. For example, you may prefer to continue with your manual accounts receivable system at the same time you are running an automated system. In this case, you would process manually each invoice, cash receipt, and adjustment in the manual system in addition to entering each item in the computerized receivables system. After a specific period of time you would compare results to confirm that they agreed.

PAPERFLOW

Implementing a computer in your organization will have a dramatic effect on the way documents flow through the company. While existing documents may be eliminated, new ones will come from the new system. Design your new paperflow procedures to determine:

- What to keep and for how long.
- What documents no longer need to be filed and how they should be destroyed.
- Where and how to file new documentation being received from the system.

Make a specific person responsible for each document prepared by the system and its ultimate filing or destruction. At the very minimum you must file all original documents (invoices, receipts, etc.) and the audit trail that refers to those documents. You should develop a process to ensure that reports are destroyed when they are no longer required. Computers are known to generate a lot of extra documents; good management of these documents will ensure they get used properly.

ACCOUNTING AND MANAGEMENT CONTROLS

Accounting and management controls are used to ensure that all information is entered into the new system and to make sure the information is complete, accurate, and authorized.

Completeness means confirming that all documents enter the system and are posted to the system. In an accounts receivable application, for instance, if all invoices are not entered into the system, they may never be collected. A common method for controlling completeness is to batch source documents and establish control totals. Batch is a term used to describe a group of documents processed at the same time. For instance, a batch might include 50 invoices from a single day's sales. A total of all the invoices (called the control total) is then determined. By comparing the control total to the total obtained from the computer, you can check that all figures were entered completely and accurately. Information regarding the batch – including batch number, date, type, and possibly the initials of the manager responsible for authorization – is entered on the batch control log, along with the totals from each one. At the end of the month, the general ledger printout shows the total debits and credits entered for the month. These figures should agree with those in the batch control log.

Accuracy involves making sure the information that is put into the system is accurate. It is important to monitor batch totals on all critical fields. Sophisticated accounting software will also have input editing procedures to ensure that information is entered accurately. For example, the system would not allow the entry of an invalid date, a vendor number that does not relate to an existing vendor, or a non-existent chart of account number.

For information to be properly **authorized**, all transactions must be approved by management.

The proper design of accounting and management controls will ensure that these three objectives are met. To function efficiently, the controls should avoid redundancy. In other words, if the system is already set up to make sure all transactions are input correctly, there is no sense adding another control with the same objective. The use of a limited number of key control points can effectively eliminate incomplete and inaccurate entry of information into the computer system.

PROCEDURES MANUALS

Manuals are used to document the procedures outlined about, including transaction processing (the entry of individual transactions), accounting and management control, back-up policies, and the flow of paper through the system. The importance of documenting these procedures cannot be overemphasized. These procedures ensure that all processing is carried out in a timely and consistent manner. Then if a key employee is absent from the job, the documentation can be used as instructions for the replacement staff. Documented procedures can also act as training manuals to help ease the problems caused by staff turnover and prolonged absences. As well, by documenting procedures that are performed only at month-end and year-end, errors can be eliminated and potential problems reduced by ensuring that all the necessary steps are taken. Finally, documented procedures can help allocate specific responsibilities to specific individuals.

Although procedures manuals can be organized in various ways, it's useful to have procedures outlined for daily, weekly, monthly, and year-end processes. These procedures manuals should not be confused with instructions found in the manual provided with the software. These procedures manuals should be specific to the use of that software in your particular business environment.

7 / Support and Maintenance

Sally's Novelty Supply, a small gift shop in Atlantic Canada, invested in a computer system to help monitor the company's inventory. Sally Martina, the owner-manager, didn't want to spend a lot of time operating the computer. All she wanted was a tool to help manage the business. She also didn't want her staff to waste time researching and supporting the new system, although she did know she'd have to get somebody to fill this role.

So Martina hired a consultant to handle the day-to-day problems arising with the computer software and arranged for her hardware vendor to ensure that the equipment was kept operational. Martina encouraged her staff to see the consultant rather than research problems on their own time.

After a year, Martina felt her staff had a good understanding of the company's software. As a result, she switched from an annual contract to an hourly agreement that charged her only for the time her consultant spent answering questions and solving problems. Martina now says that the maintenance and support contracts helped her ensure the successful implementation of the company's computer system.

However, unlike Martina, many owner-managers underestimate the importance of maintenance and support. Once installation is complete, some erroneously believe that the system will take care of itself. But computers are mechanical devices that eventually wear down. Just as you wouldn't expect a car to remain in excellent condition without regular servicing, your computer system requires similar care.

Perhaps more. Because your computer system includes a number of complex software programs, many things are capable of going wrong, not all of them mechanical. That's where software support comes in.

You will need help at other times as well. On average, only about 20 percent of the features included in popular applications like word processing and spreadsheets are regularly used by operators. But that doesn't make the other 80 percent any less important to your business. Even if you need to perform a function only once, that function is not part of the 20 percent the operator knows, performing the task will be difficult. You'll need to ask the advice of an expert. Getting software to perform exactly as expected can also be an enormous challenge. Support is needed along with training to make sure your staff can use the computer system effectively. Support is particularly important:

- If your employees are not 100 percent confident in their abilities with the computerized accounting system.
- If you use applications that can significantly affect the profitability of your organization.

Choosing the right kind of support for your hardware and software is difficult. Beginning with software support, this chapter examines the many options available to the owner-manager and points out the most appropriate alternatives.

SOFTWARE AND SUPPORT IN A BUSINESS ENVIRONMENT

During an average day, most organizations experience various technical problems and difficulties with their business software. Sometimes, these problems can be solved by an experienced co-worker. More often, it takes an expert to explain why a particular program suddenly won't run, or why a document file can no longer be accessed. As accounting programs become more sophisticated and complex, problems become increasingly commonplace. And so does the need for support.

The purpose of software support is to provide organizations with solutions to their day-to-day technical problems. It is usually provided by an independent consultant or vendor who has expertise with the software, or by the manufacturer of the product. Software support contracts do not replace the need for proper training; they serve merely as a supplement. Software support can benefit your organization in many ways:

- Reduce the time operators spend on research.
- Lower the risk of error and destruction of data.

- Lessen a company's dependence on on-site expertise.

Reduce Research

As your staff encounter unusual and unexpected problems during the day-to-day operation of your computer system, two things commonly happen. First, since your workers are bound to find these difficulties intimidating and frustrating, they become unhappy and less productive. Second, a lot of their time is spent researching a solution to each particular problem. A good consultant or a vendor who provides software support will have experience using the software in many types of businesses and has probably researched in the past the problems you are encountering. Instead of sifting through user manuals and other technical documentation, your staff can get solutions from the consultants. Since they will no longer need to spend time looking when they could be working, you will save money and increase productivity.

Lower Risk of Error

Since most software programs allow you to delete a file with a simple command, users sometimes erase by accidentally selecting the wrong command. Usually, however, the erased data can be recovered using special utility software. If it's not done properly, however, the data can become permanently lost and not even the recovery software will be effective.

When a problem occurs, there are usually a number of ways to go about finding a solution. In some cases, using the wrong approach can result in increased problems – even the total destruction of valuable data. Software support contracts give your staff the opportunity to obtain informed advice before they make critical decisions.

Lessen The Need for On-Site Expertise

The ideal individual to manage your computerized system, especially in the area of accounting, is someone whose expertise includes computers and the specific software used by your organization, as well as accounting. Most owner-managed businesses can't afford to hire this kind of qualified staff member. For them, it's more cost-effective to hire less-qualified accounting staff and rely on third-party contracts to help with the more technical aspects of the accounting implementation. The owner-manager can thus reduce salary costs without sacrificing the required expertise.

TYPES OF SUPPORT

Merlin Watson Equipment Ltd. is an owner-managed farm equipment dealer. Watson, the owner-manager, employed an accountant with excellent computer skills to prepare his financial information. Because of the demand for skilled computer professionals, Watson had to pay a large salary to keep the accountant on staff. When she left the company, Watson decided to try to save money. He hired an accountant with excellent business and bookkeeping skills but no computer experience. Watson then paid for the accountant's computer training himself. A software support contract that covered the accounting software gave the new accountant assistance whenever he experienced a problem. Meanwhile, Watson was able to save 25 percent in salary costs.

Although various types of support contracts are available, they typically fall into one of three categories:

- Unlimited annual support contract.
- Block of time services.
- Hourly contract.

Unlimited Support Contract

An unlimited support contract provides your organization with the right to make any number of calls to the consultant or vendor, usually during business hours. These contracts are typically sold on an annual basis, with charges assessed either monthly or yearly. Their main advantage is that your staff can get support whenever it is needed. Since no additional fees are charged for usage, employees feel comfortable calling whenever a problem arises, thereby reducing the risk of error and eliminating research time. Annual support contracts offer customers two options: on-site support and telephone assistance. With on-site support, the consultant visits your place of business, at your request, to solve problems. With telephone support, you are given a special "hotline" number to call whenever a problem occurs. All solutions are provided over the phone. On-site support is more expensive and is usually not offered on an unlimited basis. Rather it is generally purchased for a block of time.

Your organization should probably consider an annual support contract in the first two years following the implementation of the accounting software. During this start-up phase, when your staff will not be completely comfortable with the software, a telephone support contract will assist them on a day-to-day basis to keep the system operational. Telephone support is most effective where small, specific questions are concerned. For example, a user may be having trouble getting a document to print. Once the consultant has verified that all hardware connections are sound, the questioning will probably focus on the software. The consultant can run through a series of checks with the user. Perhaps the wrong key was selected. Perhaps the software hadn't been "told" a printing device was available. Or maybe the user selected the wrong printer definition from the software's menu. These specific areas can be covered systematically by the consultant.

If the problem persists, an on-site visit may be in order. On-site support is usually most effective when major problems are involved. If, for example, the user gets a "data error" message every time the machine is turned on, the operating system may be faulty, or the hard drive where the operating system is stored may have broken down. Often, the only way to know for sure is to test the equipment. Similarly, if data on a hard drive is accidentally erased, the consultant may have to visit in person to recover the information.

Block of Time Services

The second type of support contract usually involves the purchase of a number of hours of telephone support time. This arrangement is best if your staff are more comfortable with the software but still require assistance from time to time. Under this system, each time an employee contacts the consultants, time is used against the contract.

Hourly Contracts

With an hourly contract, your organization pays for support on an hourly basis – an effective solution when your staff are very comfortable with the computer system and the risk of error is minimal. The advantage of an hourly contract is that you pay only for time actually used. The disadvantage is that the hourly rate for this kind of support is often quite high. Because your staff may be reluctant to make use of support services, serious difficulties can occur as chronic problems go unchecked for long periods.

Proper Mix

To select the right support contract for your business, begin by reviewing each alternative and considering whether it suits your needs. Perhaps your organization would benefit from a combination of support services. For instance, if you have new software or your staff is just learning the system, you may want to use an unlimited support contract. In these early learning stages, your staff will have many questions. An unlimited support contract will encourage them to seek help because the service is already paid for. They will feel more comfortable knowing even the simplest questions won't cost the company extra money. If your staff are very confident and well trained, support is not as vital, and you may want to go with a block of time or an hourly contract. Many owner-managers prefer to use an annual telephone support contract to solve day-to-day problems and an on-site service purchased on an hourly basis in case of more serious problems.

A small diaper service located in eastern Canada implemented a general ledger, accounts receivable, and accounts payable system. The owner-manager originally wanted an unlimited, on-site support contract, which cost nearly as much as unlimited telephone support. After reviewing the situation, he agreed to purchase unlimited telephone support and on-site support on an hourly basis. During the first year, the company required only three on-site support calls for a total of 5.5 hours. By using telephone support for the bulk of its support needs, the diaper service saved nearly 50 percent on the cost of unlimited on-site support.

SELECTING A SUPPORT CONSULTANT OR VENDOR

Besides selecting the type of support that's best for you, you also have to decide which support service suits your needs. Four issues should be considered:

- The support service's familiarity with your organization.
- The support service's level of experience.
- The availability of the support.
- The cost.

Familiarity

Your support consultant must be familiar with your organization and how it operates and should demonstrate a reasonable understanding of your staff, their strengths and weaknesses, and where your organization is most likely to have problems. A variety of people who come in contact with your organization will possess the credentials you require. Your accountant, for example, may have the required expertise to qualify as a good source of support. Another excellent source of support is the consultant or vendor responsible for assisting in the conversion process discussed in Chapter 6. Few support contractors can claim to be as familiar with your organization as the vendor responsible for the successful implementation of your computer system.

Expertise

To support a computerized accounting system, the support service must have expertise in accounting, in the specific software application, and of course in computers. Similarly, if you are introducing word processing or a desktop publishing system, your support service should be expert in these fields. When selecting a support service, be sure to ask about the support staff. Do not hesitate to ask for credentials and to check references.

Availability

Also consider the support service's ability to respond promptly to your questions on an ongoing basis. Determine the service's accessibility and how long they take to respond to queries. If your business is in the first stages of computerization, immediate response time is vital. Check the service's claims with other owner-managed businesses using the company for support. The support service's location can affect availability, especially when on-site support is involved. Although many techniques are available to provide sophisticated telephone support, sooner or later your organization will require on-site service. As such, it's often preferable to use local support when it's available.

Cost

Because prices vary so dramatically from one type of service contract to another, it's important to bear in mind that the cost of support is relative to its value. When considering the cost, be sure to include such factors as:

- The cost and risk of failure.
- The cost of hiring in-house expertise.

By determining the risk of failure and estimating the costs related to that failure, you will get an idea of the value of the support. Costs usually vary depending on how long the failure lasts. In the case of the deleted batch transactions mentioned earlier, initial costs would be based on the length of time it would take to recreate the data. Assuming an employee spends a day entering the data and earns $15 an hour, the basic cost is $120. That doesn't include the initial time spent trying to recover the data (perhaps three hours), help received from other employees (perhaps one hour each from two co-workers also earning $15 an hour), or involvement of the supervisor or manager. These are just the tangible costs. Hidden costs include the loss of productivity that results during the time the information is not available to the organization. Perhaps the information is needed so other employees can complete their jobs. Perhaps a financial report is late getting to the bank because the information is not available. Finally, you have to consider each employee's contribution to the company's overall profit. If an employee is unable to perform a task because information is unavailable, what effect does this have on the bottom line? A failure that starts out with a price tag of $250 to $300 can soon end up costing your organization hundreds or thousands of dollars more.

MAINTENANCE

Maintenance is the upkeep of hardware and software. Many owner-managed businesses regard maintenance as a type of insurance and pay a fixed rate to ensure that their machines are kept in working order whether or not repairs are needed. The alternative is to pay only when the machine breaks down, which in many businesses poses a risk not worth taking. A machine that breaks down once during the year can often cost more to fix than it would to insure the unit under a service arrangement.

SOFTWARE MAINTENANCE

Software developers are constantly upgrading their pre-packaged software products in an attempt to improve performance and market share. Maintenance usually involves replacing an existing product with an improved version. In a payroll system, for instance, maintenance contracts usually include automatic updates to the annual tax tables required for your payroll system. Not so with custom-written software. Because custom software is subject to more problems and errors than off-the-shelf products, and because there is no automatic mechanism to have these problems cleared up by the developer, you should always negotiate at least a one-year maintenance contract to ensure acceptable performance. The one-year contract should take your organization through all cycles of the software to make sure all the features and commands built into the package work as they were intended. A general ledger system, for example, should be tested to make sure the daily processing and monthly and yearly cycles all perform to expectation. Because the yearly cycle is run only once a year, it can take your company that long to determine if the software performs according to expectations.

HARDWARE MAINTENANCE

Although hardware is becoming increasingly reliable, a computer system is still a mechanical device. And mechanical devices are subject to wear and breakdown. It's therefore just a matter of time before your hardware will require maintenance and servicing. The decision to purchase a maintenance contract for your computer should be based on how comfortable you are living with the risk of potential equipment malfunctions. Although some organizations have demonstrated that it's more cost-effective to operate without a maintenance contract, in the majority of cases maintenance proves to be a cost-saving measure.

When selecting a hardware maintenance vendor, your organization should consider these four questions:

- What are the technician's credentials and qualifications?
- Does the vendor have the appropriate documentation and service manuals for your equipment?
- Does the vendor have the necessary parts?
- Does the vendor own diagnostic equipment to run tests on your hardware?

Before you allow a technician to take apart your hardware, be sure to ask for his or her qualifications. You may have to base your assessment on the technician's past experience, since the occupation is essentially unregulated. Provincial associations of certified electronics technologists do exist, but enrolment is not mandatory. Currently, technicians require no special credentials to work on microcomputers.

The service vendor should have on hand the proper service documentation and technical manuals for your equipment. Without the right technical documentation, your vendor will have a difficult time providing reliable support.

Your service organization should have access to spare parts required for your particular hardware. Critical parts should be kept in stock for emergencies.

Finally, a good service organization should have sufficient diagnostic equipment to test circuits, to make sure connections are sound, and to test equipment such as hard drives and printing devices. Without diagnostic equipment, the technician will find it difficult to pinpoint a problem quickly and accurately. Making sure that your vendor has the proper diagnostic equipment can help prevent lengthy service calls.

In addition, you may want to check references with other owner-managed businesses using the same support organization. Often, personal references can tell you more about the organization than asking the vendor the four questions outlined above.

ON-SITE VERSUS CARRY-IN

When you purchase hardware maintenance services, you have your choice of on-site support, in which a technician visits your business in the event of a problem, or a "carry-in" arrangement. With a carry-in contract, you're responsible for delivering the hardware to the service centre for repairs. Many people believe that faster results can be obtained through on-site support, and they're prepared to pay significantly more for it. However, carry-in support is sometimes faster because the technician has immediate access to all the parts, documentation, and diagnostic equipment necessary to service the equipment.

PREVENTIVE MAINTENANCE

All systems require some form of preventive maintenance, and your service vendor should provide it on a semi-annual basis. Generally, such maintenance involves checking hard drives to make sure they aren't in danger of failing, cleaning keyboards, removing dust from the units, and so on. If a piece of the equipment is likely to fail, the vendor will replace it to eliminate the risk of serious problems further down the road. It's like servicing your car.

INSURANCE

Your computer system and the information contained within it are valuable assets. Check that your insurance covers the equipment. Also, depending on the type of information stored on the system, you may want to consider business disruption insurance. Some organizations, for example, depend completely on computerized information. If the information is lost, the company can't function. If, for example, an airline loses its reservation system, it cannot do business, since the reservation is equivalent to an order that's been placed in a merchandising environment. By insuring the data against possible loss, the company receives compensation if it's unable to continue doing business for any length of time.

8/Staff Issues and Outside Help

Implementing a computer system is an enormous task and calls for input from any number of experts, including vendors, accountants, and software programmers. Although you will make the final decisions, you should be aware of the valuable contribution that outside help can provide to the decision-making process. This section will identify when it is best to use outside help.

SETTING OBJECTIVES

Only you and your staff can decide what you expect computerization to do since no one else knows your business as well or understands its plans. However, you may want to ask an outside consultant for help in identifying additional benefits that may apply to your organization. Good outside consultants are aware of the latest technology and have experience working in various industries and in other organizations in your own industry. They can point out where a computer system can and cannot assist you in your work.

Review your objectives with your accountant or computer consultant only after you and your staff are satisfied with the goals you have set. In this way you will quickly benefit from the expertise of others without having to pay for work you could do yourself. If, for example, you want to automate your inventory control but are unaware of the work involved, an experienced consultant can draw on past knowledge to help you make up your mind. A consultant can also recommend which items should be tracked in inventory and which should be tracked manually.

You should also define your organization's needs. Even if a consultant contributes to the task by interviewing your staff, your involvement will still be required. In most cases, you can save time by completing pre-developed checklists such as those found in Chapter

3. You should have your consultant review the completed checklists to ensure that they are complete and appropriate for your organization. As discussed in Chapter 3, this step is critical in the selection of the right computer system for your business.

SOFTWARE SELECTION

Determining which software package will satisfy your needs can be accomplished most efficiently by your computer consultant. For one thing, trying to evaluate all the accounting and business software packages applicable to your business can be extremely time-consuming. While software vendors usually have the knowledge and expertise necessary to recommend a system, their suggestions are often limited to the stock they carry. Only a consultant is in a position to objectively evaluate all possible software solutions. An independent consultant familiar with the accounting packages being reviewed can most efficiently identify which of your needs will be satisfied by each of the packages under review.

You can significantly reduce your consultant's time by restricting the number of packages you want reviewed. In most cases, your consultant should be able to help you shortlist those packages that are most likely to meet your needs. Be sure to discuss this with your consultant before asking that a large number of programs be reviewed.

HARDWARE SELECTION

As discussed in Chapter 4, once the software has been selected, your options regarding hardware and operating systems will be limited. Have your consultant review the hardware specifications to ensure that the needs of your organization are being met. For example, if you're taking telephone orders and giving customers information over the telephone, you'll require hardware that is fast enough to allow your staff to respond to the customer requests in as little time as possible. Your consultant would be able to advise of the type of hardware necessary to achieve the required retrieval speed. Aside from this, the selection of a particular brand of equipment is a matter of personal choice. Your computer consultant probably purchases many systems on behalf of clients and may have arrangements with several vendors in your area to obtain better pricing. However, if the consultant receives commission on the sale of a particular brand of hardware, the possibility of receiving an objective recommendation is less likely. Be sure to ask your consultant or accountant of all vendor arrangements well in advance. In some cases, the consultant's business connections can help you save money on the computer equipment.

TRAINING

Unless your organization is very large, chances are you'll benefit more by having the training performed outside the company, since most people are better able to learn radically new concepts and ideas when they're outside their normal work environment. Taking people outside the organization for training allows them to view the job they do from an outsider's perspective, making them better able to adapt to a computerized system. If you elect to do on-the-job-training without hiring professionals, you'll need to put together a detailed training plan that identifies where you expect to obtain the materials necessary for the task, such as training manuals, audio-visual equipment, workbooks, and so on. If you choose this approach, your consultant can help you develop an effective plan.

CONVERSION/IMPLEMENTATION

Conversion/Implementation is another critical area that can benefit from the assistance of an outside consultant. Chapter 6 outlines many specific areas that require a high level of technical expertise, such as data back-up procedures, designing the chart of account, and developing paperflow procedures. When planning the conversion of your accounting system, ensure that the consultant is responsible for all tasks related to design and control, such as batch processes and monthly financial statements. You and your staff should be responsible for all data entry and more mundane conversion tasks. You can save your organization money by entering data and by coming up with the opening balance, setting up customer accounts, and so on. In cases where a lot of data entry is required, you may find it useful to use temporary office help to supplement existing staff. Many companies find this tactic necessary when introducing an inventory control system, which typically requires an enormous amount of data entry.

SUPPORT AND MAINTENANCE

Software support and hardware maintenance are normally provided by outside consultants. Since most small businesses are not large enough to dedicate a staff member to just support and maintenance, these services are usually purchased from outside. Chapter 7 points out several techniques your organization can use to reduce the cost of support and maintenance contracts.

SELECTING THE RIGHT CONSULTANT FOR YOUR ORGANIZATION

When selecting a consultant to assist you with the computerization of your organization, consider several factors:

- What skills does the consultant have?
- How wide is the consultant's experience?
- Will you get value for money spent?
- Is the consultant associated with any particular computer company?

Skills

A good consultant has a variety of skills. You should be primarily concerned with the consultant's skills in three areas:

- Business expertise.
- Knowledge of specific software applications.
- Knowledge of computers.

Business skills should be your main concern. Understanding how computers work is naturally important, but in the long run the computer's work is to help you manage your business more effectively. Unless your consultant understands accounting issues and your business, he or she won't be able to figure out how a computer can best help you achieve your goals and objectives, and you could end up paying for a poorly designed system that provides only basic information, or worse, with an automated system that doesn't work at all. If possible, choose a consultant who has experience in your industry. Ideally, choose one with prior experience with your organization.

Ask potential consultants which application software they have worked with. If they have experience and training in various software, they are more likely to be successful in computerizing your organization, and they will also spend less time on the project. Also be sure to check references. Without some kind of testimonial from satisfied clients, you can't be sure the consultant is capable of meeting your needs. A manufacturing organization recently discovered the importance of references when it hired a consultant to automate the company. The project was complicated, involving inventory control, an accounting system, and a manufacturing system. It also required an expensive minicomputer, rather than a micro-based machine. Initially, the consultant impressed the owner-manager with a long string of engineering and software programming credentials. Business credentials were few and far between. But the owner-manager, thinking the consultant had all the technical expertise necessary to undertake such a difficult project, wasn't concerned. The consultant was engaged to do the job. The consultant started with the accounting system and immediately ran into trouble. After two-and-a-half years, the system still wasn't operational. Finally, the owner-manager fired the consultant and tried to win back damages by filing a lawsuit. Had the company run a thorough reference check, the consultant's weakness would have been revealed.

Finally, you should ensure that your consultant has a good general understanding of computers and a good working knowledge of the operating systems your organization will be using. Most owner-managers don't want to waste time installing programs, creating directories and sub-directories, formatting hard drives, and so on. Usually, a basic understanding of DOS commands (in the IBM environment) such as delete, copy, and erase is as much as the owner-manager wants to know.

Experience

Because the successful implementation of your accounting system depends in no small part on the consultant's intimate knowledge of your business, using only one consultant or consulting company for all phases of the implementation process yields the best results. Therefore, it's best if the consultant's organization is capable of providing all the services you will require during the implementation of your computer, from needs analysis and software selection all the way to conversion and ongoing support.

Value

Just as in most things in life, when you employ an outside consultant, you get what you pay for. However, you should be certain that your consultant makes every effort to be cost-effective when dealing with your organization. A good consultant will perform only the tasks that you can't do yourself. Anything that involves simple data entry, for example, should be done by your staff. If certain tasks can be performed by you in advance, the consultant should tell you, so little time will be wasted. In other words, a good consultant knows how to make effective use of time. Remember that your overall objective is to get the computer system up and running. Your consultant's role is to improve the probability of success in this endeavour. Keep this in mind when considering the cost of using an outside consultant.

Independence

Because the computer industry is so specialized, individual consultants often concentrate on specific software packages in order to maintain a reasonable level of expertise. When selecting a consultant, ask what software he or she has experience with and the depth of experience of his or her organization.

Many software vendors are in the habit of offering commissions to consultants who recommend their software. You should know, in advance, whether your consultant is receiving commissions, since it might affect his or her judgement when recommending a particular system.

After you have selected a consultant, ask for a written contract or engagement letter clearly outlining the consultant's responsibilities and fees.

9 / Estimating the Cost

Only if you know in advance how much your computer system is going to cost can you determine how quickly you will be able to implement your computer plan and how it will affect your cash flow. A cost estimate will also provide you with a sound and reasonable budget to show your banker if you need to obtain additional financing.

While you're planning your software and hardware requirements, determining your training needs, and setting up your conversion schedule, you should be making rough cost estimates. These estimates will help you decide how far you can go with your computerization plan without unduly stretching your company's finances. Eventually you will have to convert the rough estimates into an accurate assessment of your financial requirements to make sure you're prepared for every eventuality.

THE COSTING PHASE

When estimating costs, break your plan into phases and focus on one phase at a time. The phases used for costing should be aligned with the implementation phases of your conversion plan. If a phase extends over your company's financial year-end, you may want to split it into two sub-phases to allow you to assess costs for each financial year for budgeting and reporting purposes.

SOFTWARE COSTS

In most cases, companies don't buy software. Rather, they obtain programs and a licence for their use. Each program comes with a licence agreement set out by the software publisher. The terms of the agreement tend to vary from package to package, and from publisher to publisher. Normally, software licence agreements drafted for standalone versions include provisions that limit the number of copies that can be made and permit the use of the software on a single machine only. More permissive agreements allow the software to be moved freely from one computer to another, as long as the program isn't run on more than one computer at a time. In a similar way, LAN software may require that individual users are licenced, or alternatively that the network is licenced for a certain number of simultaneous users. To determine how many copies of the software you'll require, you have to check the terms of the agreement.

Once you've determined how many copies of each type of software you need, you will be able to estimate your total software costs. Remember that the price of software packages often depends on your ability to negotiate discounts from the vendor. Most software comes with a suggested list price, but remember that these prices often don't include delivery or installation on your computer.

Your Organization
Computerization Plan
Cost Estimates

	Phase 1	Phase 2	Phase 3	Cost
Software:				
General ledger (upgrade)	XXX			XXX
Accounts Receivable (upgrade)	XXX			XXX
Retail Invoicing (upgrade)	XXX			XXX
Accounts Payable	XXX			XXX
Lotus	XXX			XXX
Quik Reports		XXX		XXX
Windowing System Manager		XXX		XXX
Novell Advanced 286		XXX		XXX
Lanpak (8 units)		XXX		XXX
Inventory Control			XXX	XXX
Order Entry			XXX	XXX
Purchase Orders			XXX	XXX
	XXX	XXX	XXX	XXX

Hardware				
Compaq 386(110 Meg HD/ 2 Meg RAM/Arcnet Card/DOS 4.01)		XXX		XXX
3 – Compaq 286 (20 Meg HD/ 1 Meg Ram/Arcnet Card)	XXX		XXX	XXX
4 – Monitors	XXX	XXX	XXX	XXX
3 – Arcnet cards (existing workstations)		XXX		XXX
120 meg Techmar Tape Backup		XXX		XXX
520 Watt UPS		XXX		XXX
	XXX	XXX	XXX	XXX
Conversion				
General Ledger	XXX			XXX
Accounts Receivable	XXX			XXX
Accounts Payable	XXX			XXX
Novell		XXX		XXX
Inventory Control			XXX	XXX
Order Entry			XXX	XXX
Purchase Orders			XXX	XXX
	XXX	XXX	XXX	XXX
	Phase 1	Phase 2	Phase 3	Cost
Training				
Intro to Micros (5 days)	XXX		XXX	XXX
Word Perfect (2 days)	XXX			XXX
Intro Lotus (4 days)	XXX			XXX
General Ledger (6 days)	XXX			XXX
Accounts Receivable (2 days)	XXX			XXX
Accounts Payable (2 days)	XXX			XXX
dBASE (2 days)	XXX			XXX
Network Supervisor training		XXX		XXX
Inventory Control (2 days)			XXX	XXX
Order Entry (1 day)			XXX	XXX
	XXX	XXX	XXX	XXX
Total (not including sales tax)	XXX	XXX	XXX	XXX

The above cost does not include the cost of cabling. The recommended coaxial cable is $2/foot. Your organization is responsible for the installation of the cable. The vendor is responsible for the terminating of cable ends and the connection of the workstations to the server.

Annual Support Costs				
Hardware (per YR/2 YR Cont)	XXX	XXX	XXX	XXX
Application Support	XXX	XXX	XXX	XXX
	XXX	XXX	XXX	XXX

The costs of custom software development should be negotiated with the developer. It's usually best to have a fixed price contract with specified deliverables agreed to by both parties. The example of a computerization plan cost estimate section set out in Table 9.1 illustrates how software costs would be allocated to the particular phase of the conversion process.

HARDWARE COSTS

Hardware costs are usually estimated separately for each system component such as:

- Microcomputer units.
- Monitors.
- Printers.
- Network interface cards.
- Tape back-up units.

As part of your planning process, you'll have already determined your hardware requirements. These requirements will include the information you need to determine pricing for each kind of computer you require.

Most hardware vendors carry a number of standard units. If you have any special requirements, these should be taken into consideration when estimating your costs. To make sure your results are complete and accurate, supply your vendor with detailed specifications, setting out the exact requirements of each unit you're purchasing. For example, some microcomputer units come with monitor interfaces and printer ports, while others charge extra for these features. Ensuring that all the necessary components are included in the price is the most difficult and confusing part of this exercise.

As you did with software, you can use your negotiating skills to obtain discounts from the various vendors. Get quotations from several dealers to make sure you have the best possible deal. Most microcomputers are also offered at "bargain basement" prices advertised in the local press. But these prices do not include everything; you may have to pay for delivery, hook-up, hard disk formatting, and software installation.

Once you have a quotation from your hardware suppliers, you'll be able to break your cost estimates down by implementation phase as set out in Table 9.1. (This table doesn't include network cabling costs, since cable is frequently installed by an electrical contractor or by building personnel. After determining how much installation will cost, you should include it in your overall estimate.)

CONVERSION COSTS

Conversion costs depend to a certain extent on the amount of outside assistance the process requires. If you expect to carry out the conversion without outside assistance, your costs will be limited to paying overtime to employees who perform after-hours tasks such as repricing, physical inventory, inputting master file information, parallel processing, and running test data. Your staff may also have to work extra hours just to become familiar with the new system. If your conversion requires assistance from an outside consultant, the costs should include the consultant's fee estimate for each sub-phase of the process.

Frequently, a consultant and/or an accountant is needed to help design the chart of accounts and set up account codes for customers, vendors, and inventory items. In addition, you may use a consultant to set up word processing forms and other applications, to install and set up the network and its procedures, and to design back-up procedures. A consultant can be hired as a project manager to supervise and manage the entire conversion.

Your company's conversion costs, including the arrangements you make with your staff, your vendors, and your consultants, should be included in your computerization plan.

TRAINING COSTS

The cost of training your personnel will be a healthy chunk of the overall computerization price tag. In most cases, your computerization plan will include only the out-of-pocket costs associated with implementing your plan. The "soft costs" of reduced productivity while staff are attending training sessions and familiarizing themselves with your new system are typically not included.

Training costs are usually determined by calculating the number of training days required for each course selected – from computer and application training to business and accounting instruction. Costs will naturally vary from vendor to vendor, and pricing discounts can usually be negotiated, depending on the amount of business you have to offer. In some cases, government funding may be available to offset some of the training costs.

ONGOING COSTS

A separate part of your computerization plan estimates should include estimates of ongoing costs, including maintenance and support fees.

Estimates of hardware maintenance costs are usually obtained from hardware vendors or specialized organizations. Annual contracts are available in addition to those that provide "guaranteed maintenance" for a number of years. Once you've established the kind you need, you should obtain quotations from a number of vendors and build the costs into your computerization plan.

When it comes to software, a number of levels of support are available. These vary from "hotline" services to program updates. Again, your computerization plan should include estimates of the costs for the particular services you require.

EVALUATE THE RESULTS

Costs can be a limiting factor when implementing a computer system and can directly influence such things as the timing, type, and extent of computerization. If you find your needs are greater or less than the funds available to you, you may have to reconsider certain elements of your plan, such as timing and the type of computer required. For example, you may decide to extend the time period for implementation so you can spread the costs over a greater period of time. Or, if your financial resources allow, you may decide to accelerate training and the implementation process.

If you change the timing of any stage, you will shift costs between phases and your cash flow will naturally be affected.

Obviously, changing the scope of your computer system will have an effect on the total cost estimate.

CONCLUSION

You always get what you pay for. If you have limited funds, you are wise to do a good job on a portion of the total system than to try to implement the entire system "on the cheap." If you implement good quality hardware and software you will be able to expand on the system later when you can afford it. If you implement a poor system, you may have to start all over again at a later date.

Good luck!

Appendix

Software Requirements Checklists

These software requirements checklists are examples of some of the checklists available to help you select appropriate software. The checklists are not necessarily all-inclusive. Be sure to add any identified needs that are specific to your organization.

The checklists include four columns: the first two columns are for your use when identifying your needs. If the information or a process is mandatory, indicate this fact with a check in the mandatory column. If the information or process is not mandatory, indicate its level of desirability in the second column by entering a number from 1 to 3 with 3 being the most desirable and 1 being the least desirable.

After you have identified all of your needs, you will compare these needs to available packages. As you evaluate the packages, use columns three and four to document whether the package can meet the requirements identified. If you are evaluating more than two packages, add columns on the right hand side.

To select the appropriate package, review the mandatory items first. After the mandatory, determine which packages meet the needs identified as desirable. In many cases workarounds will be required to meet some of the identified mandatory requirements. A consultant familiar with the package can help you to determine what workarounds are available.

Table 1
SOFTWARE REQUIREMENTS – GENERAL LEDGER

	Required		Available	
	Mandatory	Desirable	#1	#2
1. SYSTEM CAPACITY				
1.1. Maximum Number of				
Accounts	______	______	______	______
Departments	______	______	______	______
Transaction:				
• Periods	______	______	______	______
• Yearly	______	______	______	______
• History	______	______	______	______
• Accounting periods	______	______	______	______
2. DATA FILES				
2.1. Chart of Accounts				
Alphanumeric account number	______	______	______	______
Maximum number of digits:				
• Expense code	______	______	______	______
• Department code	______	______	______	______
• Cost centre code	______	______	______	______
Length of description field	______	______	______	______
Statistical accounts	______	______	______	______
Budget information:				
• Current year annual	______	______	______	______
• Current year by period	______	______	______	______
• Prior year annual	______	______	______	______
• Prior year by period	______	______	______	______
Historical data:				
• Prior year actual	______	______	______	______
2.2. Transactions				
Automatically generated system transaction number	______	______	______	______
Period number	______	______	______	______
Source code	______	______	______	______
Transaction date	______	______	______	______
Reference code	______	______	______	______
Description field:				
• Number of characters	______	______	______	______
• Multiple lines	______	______	______	______

3. PROCESSING

3.1. Enter Transactions

Description carried forward from previous transaction				
Online edit for:				
• Account number				
• Department number				
• Cost centre number				
• Source code				
• Valid date				
• Valid period				
Add new accounts during transaction entry				
Recurring entries:				
• Fixed amount				
Reversing entries				
Pre-defined payroll journal				
On-screen batch total information				
Current year				
Prior year				
User-defined period				
All accounts				
User-specified accounts				

3.2. Posting and Closing

Post to:				
• Current period				
• Period in next fiscal year				
• Period in prior fiscal year				
Batches must be balanced before posting				
Audit trails must be printed before posting				
Year-end close procedure:				
• Generates closing journal entry				
• Generates opening balances				
• Updates history				

3.3. Consolidating Companies

Consolidate companies by:				
• All companies				

- Selected companies
- Companies with different chart of accounts

3.4. <u>Edit Budget Information</u>

Edit based on prior year budget:

- Growth factor
- Incremental

Edit based on prior year actual:

- Growth factor
- Incremental

Edit based on other accounts:

- Growth factor
- Incremental

4. INQUIRY

4.1. <u>View Transactions Information</u>

- By account number
- By account description
- By source code
- By date
- Current year
- Prior year

4.2. <u>View Budget Data</u>

- Current year
- Prior year

5. REPORTING

5.1. <u>Standard Reports</u>

Chart of Accounts:

- By account
- By department
- For range of account and department numbers

Trial Balance worksheet:

- By account
- By department
- For range of account and department numbers

General Ledger detail:

- By account
- By department

• For range of account and department numbers				
• For range of periods				
Batch listing				
Batch status report				
5.2. <u>User-Defined Reports</u>				
Departmental reporting:				
• By department				
• By range of department				
Form specifications:				
• Form size				
• Page numbering				
• Page heading				
• Dollar size				
• Rounding				
Columns information from profit and loss statement:				
• Maximum number of columns				
• Current month actual				
• Current quarter to date actual				
• Current half year to date actual				
• Current year to date actual				
• Previous month actual				
• Previous quarter actual				
• Previous half year actual				
• Previous total year actual				
• Same month last year actual				
• Same quarter to date last year actual				
• Same half year to date last year actual				
• Year to date last year actual				
• Budget for current month				
• Budget for quarter date				
• Budget for half year to date				
• Budget for the year to date				
• Budget for same month last year				
• Budget for same quarter to date last year				

• Budget for same half year to date last year	______	______	______	______
• Budget for last year to date	______	______	______	______
Columns information for Balance Sheet:				
• Current balance	______	______	______	______
• Balance at beginning of month	______	______	______	______
• Balance X months ago	______	______	______	______
• Balance at beginning of quarter	______	______	______	______
• Current year opening balance	______	______	______	______
• Last year opening balance	______	______	______	______
Accumulators:				
• Ability to add columns	______	______	______	______
• Ability to carry totals forward from schedules	______	______	______	______
General:				
• Prepare graphic analysis	______	______	______	______
• Print to screen	______	______	______	______

Table 2

SOFTWARE REQUIREMENTS – ACCOUNTS RECEIVABLE

	Required		Available	
	Mandatory	**Desirable**	**#1**	**#2**
1. SYSTEM CAPACITY				
1.1. Maximum Number of:				
Customers	______	______	______	______
Transactions	______	______	______	______
Sales distribution codes	______	______	______	______
Control accounts	______	______	______	______
Bank accounts	______	______	______	______
2. DATA FILES				
2.1. Customer Files				
Customer number	______	______	______	______
Name	______	______	______	______
Address	______	______	______	______
Postal code	______	______	______	______

Telephone				
Fax				
Contact				
Salesperson				
Territory				
Credit rating				
Credit limit				
Credit hold flag				
Sales:				
• Current period				
• Year to date				
• Prior year				
• Prior year by period				
Gross profit:				
• Current period				
• Year to date				
• Year to date by period				
• Prior year				
• Prior year by period				
Date account opened				
Last sales date				
Last sales amount				
Last payment date				
Last payment amount:				
• Year to date payments				
• Year to date number of invoices				
• Prior year payments				
• Prior year number of invoices				
Statement option				
Unpaid finance charges				
Year to date finance charges				
Prior year finance charges				
Number of times past due				
Balance due				
Maximum balance				
Average balance				
Average days to pay				
Layaway information				
Accounts receivable control account				

2.2. <u>Customer File for Order Entry</u>

Ship to locations:

- One
- Many

Pricing code

Trade discount amount

Terms

Tax jurisdiction code

Tax exempt number

Amount on order

Number of invoice copies required

Customer type

Ship via method

Total commissions paid

2.3. <u>Transaction Information</u>

Customer number

Invoice/cheque number

Date

Reference number

Distribution code

Amount

3. PROCESSING

3.1. <u>Opening Amounts</u>

Enter starting invoices:

- In detail
- Opening balances only

3.2. <u>Processing Methods</u>

Account types:

- Open item
- Balance forward
- Instalment
- Revolving

3.3. <u>Invoice Entry</u>

Customer number checked for validity

Valid date check

Forced printing of audit trail

Recurring invoices

Ability to add customers from invoice entry screen

Ability to post invoices to specific periods ______ ______ ______ ______

Interface with job cost software:

- Job ______ ______ ______ ______
- Phase ______ ______ ______ ______
- Sub-phase ______ ______ ______ ______

3.4. <u>Cash Receipts</u>

Customer number checked for validity ______ ______ ______ ______

Valid date check ______ ______ ______ ______

Cash allocation

- User-specified invoices and balances ______ ______ ______ ______
- Partial payments ______ ______ ______ ______
- Pre-payments ______ ______ ______ ______
- Overpayments ______ ______ ______ ______

Ability to post receipts to specific invoices ______ ______ ______ ______

Forced printing of audit trail ______ ______ ______ ______

3.5. <u>Adjustments</u>

Automatic generation of unique system transaction number ______ ______ ______ ______

Customer number checked for validity ______ ______ ______ ______

Valid date check ______ ______ ______ ______

Batch forced to balance before posting ______ ______ ______ ______

3.6. <u>Automatic Charges</u>

Interest charges:

- By range of customer number ______ ______ ______ ______

Recurring charges ______ ______ ______ ______

3.7. <u>General</u>

End of period ______ ______ ______ ______

End of year ______ ______ ______ ______

Purge paid accounts ______ ______ ______ ______

Force print of audit trail ______ ______ ______ ______

Force print of master file change report ______ ______ ______ ______

On-screen batch total for data entry verification ______ ______ ______ ______

Automatic generation of unique system transaction number _____ _____ _____ _____

Interface with:

- General Ledger _____ _____ _____ _____
- Job Costing _____ _____ _____ _____

4. INQUIRY

4.1. Customer Information

Customer charges and payments by:

- Customer number _____ _____ _____ _____
- Invoice range _____ _____ _____ _____

Review customer information:

- By name _____ _____ _____ _____
- By number _____ _____ _____ _____
- Year to date sales:
  - total _____ _____ _____ _____
  - by period _____ _____ _____ _____
- Prior year to date sales:
  - total _____ _____ _____ _____
  - by period _____ _____ _____ _____
- Last invoice:
  - date _____ _____ _____ _____
  - amount _____ _____ _____ _____
- Last payment:
  - date _____ _____ _____ _____
  - amount _____ _____ _____ _____
- Average number of days to pay _____ _____ _____ _____

Ageing:

- User-specified periods _____ _____ _____ _____
- Summary _____ _____ _____ _____
- Detail _____ _____ _____ _____

5. REPORTING

5.1. Standard Reports

Trial Balance:

- Detail _____ _____ _____ _____
- Summary _____ _____ _____ _____
- By range of customer number _____ _____ _____ _____
- By control account _____ _____ _____ _____
- By customer balance:
  - debit balances only _____ _____ _____ _____

• credit balances only				
• User-specified ageing periods				
• Includes:				
• customer contact				
• phone number				
• customer statistics				
Customer list:				
• By range of customer number				
• By control account				
Customer statistics:				
• By range of customer number				
• By control account				
Credit limit exception report:				
• By user-defined exception amount				
• By range of customer number				
Collection report:				
• By range of customer number				
Cash flow projection report				
5.2. <u>User-Specified Reports</u>				
Customer statements:				
• Customer information				
• Invoice date				
• Invoice number				
• Transaction type				
• Invoice amount				
• Statement total				
• Ageing amounts				
• Minimum amount due				
• Messages				
Dunning letters				
Mailing labels				

Table 3
SOFTWARE REQUIREMENTS – ACCOUNTS PAYABLE

	Required		Available	
	Mandatory	**Desirable**	**#1**	**#2**
1. SYSTEM CAPACITY				
1.1. Maximum number of:				
Customers				
Transactions				
Control accounts				
Bank accounts				
2. DATA FILES				
2.1. Vendor File				
Vendor number				
Name				
Address				
Postal code				
Telephone				
Fax				
Contact				
Hold payment status				
Default due date				
Default terms				
Control account				
Alternate payee				
Purchases history:				
• Year to date purchases				
• Year to date discounts taken				
• Year to date discounts missed				
• Year to date finance charges				
• Prior year purchases				
• Prior year discounts taken				
• Prior year discounts missed				
• Prior year finance charges				
Payment history:				
• Last payment date				
• Last cheque number				
• Last transaction date				
Prepaid amounts				

2.2. Transaction Date

Vendor number ____ ____ ____ ____
Invoice number ____ ____ ____ ____
Date ____ ____ ____ ____
Reference number ____ ____ ____ ____
P.O. number ____ ____ ____ ____
P.O. date ____ ____ ____ ____
Tax information:
- Provincial Sales Tax ____ ____ ____ ____
- Federal Sales Tax ____ ____ ____ ____
- Goods and Services Tax ____ ____ ____ ____

Freight ____ ____ ____ ____
Total due ____ ____ ____ ____
Cheque number ____ ____ ____ ____
Bank account ____ ____ ____ ____
Buyer ____ ____ ____ ____
History:
- Open invoices only ____ ____ ____ ____
- All invoices and payments:
  - current period ____ ____ ____ ____
  - current year to date ____ ____ ____ ____
  - user defined period ____ ____ ____ ____

3. PROCESSING

3.1. Opening Amounts

Enter starting payables:
- Detail ____ ____ ____ ____
- Balance forward only ____ ____ ____ ____

3.2. Processing Methods

Accounting options:
- Accrual basis ____ ____ ____ ____
- Cash basis ____ ____ ____ ____

3.3. Invoice Entry

Automatic check for duplicate invoices ____ ____ ____ ____
Automatic assignment of default terms ____ ____ ____ ____
- One account ____ ____ ____ ____
- Prorated to many accounts ____ ____ ____ ____

Online edit of:
- Vendor number ____ ____ ____ ____

- Invoice date ______ ______ ______ ______
- Due date ______ ______ ______ ______
- General Ledger account codes ______ ______ ______ ______

Ability to prorate:

- Discounts ______ ______ ______ ______
- Taxes ______ ______ ______ ______
- Freight ______ ______ ______ ______
- Finance charges ______ ______ ______ ______

Recurring monthly payments ______ ______ ______ ______

3.4. <u>Cheque-Processing</u>

Payment control:

- By invoice ______ ______ ______ ______
- By vendor ______ ______ ______ ______
- Place invoice on hold:
  - indefinitely ______ ______ ______ ______
  - until next payment cycle ______ ______ ______ ______
  - by invoices ______ ______ ______ ______
  - by vendors ______ ______ ______ ______
- Force invoice payment ______ ______ ______ ______
- Change invoice maximum payment ______ ______ ______ ______
- Change invoice discount base ______ ______ ______ ______
- Change invoice due date ______ ______ ______ ______
- Partial payments on specified invoices ______ ______ ______ ______

Pre-cheque register:

- Automatic calculation of discounts and finance charges:
  - manual override ______ ______ ______ ______
- Automatic payment:
  - by discount date ______ ______ ______ ______
  - by due date ______ ______ ______ ______
  - all invoices ______ ______ ______ ______
  - specified invoices ______ ______ ______ ______
  - all but specified invoices ______ ______ ______ ______
  - specified vendors ______ ______ ______ ______
  - all but specified vendors ______ ______ ______ ______

Pay multiple invoices with the cheque:

- From one location ______ ______ ______ ______

- From multiple locations
- From multiple cost centres

Pay from different banks as specified in vendor record

Process pre-payments

Manual cheques:

- Single cheques
- Batches
- Distribute to General Ledger
- Allocate to job costing

3.5. Adjustment Entry

Online edit of:

- Vendor number
- Date

Batch forced to balance before posting

3.6. General

Interface with:

- General Ledger
- Purchasing/receiving
- Job Costing
- Order Entry

Bank reconciliation

Forced printing of audit trail

On-screen batch total for data entry verification

Post to user-specified accounting period:

- By batch
- By invoice
- Process foreign currency invoices

4. INQUIRY

4.1. Vendor Information

Invoices and payments by:

- Vendor number
- Vendor name

Review vendor information:

- By name

• By number	______	______	______	______
• Year to date purchases	______	______	______	______
• Prior year purchases	______	______	______	______
• Year to date discounts taken	______	______	______	______
• Prior year discounts taken	______	______	______	______
• Year to date discounts missed	______	______	______	______
• Prior year discounts missed	______	______	______	______
• Last invoice:				
• date	______	______	______	______
• amount	______	______	______	______
• Last payment:				
• date	______	______	______	______
• amount	______	______	______	______

5. REPORTING

5.1. Standard Reports

Vendor list:				
• By range of vendor number	______	______	______	______
• By control account	______	______	______	______
• Alphabetical order	______	______	______	______
• Vendor number order	______	______	______	______
Vendor statistics:				
• By range of vendor number	______	______	______	______
• By control account	______	______	______	______
Detailed open payables:				
• By range of vendor number	______	______	______	______
• By control account	______	______	______	______
• User-specified ageing periods	______	______	______	______
• By due date	______	______	______	______
• By discount date	______	______	______	______
• By invoice date	______	______	______	______
Overdue payables listing:				
• By range of vendor number	______	______	______	______
• By control account	______	______	______	______
• User-defined ageing periods	______	______	______	______
• In summary	______	______	______	______
• In detail	______	______	______	______
Report identifying future cash requirements:				
• By range of vendor number	______	______	______	______
• By control account	______	______	______	______

• User-defined ageing periods				
• Include discounts option				
• Include hold payments option				
• In summary				
• In detail				
Posting journals				
Pre-cheque register:				
• By range of vendors				
Cheque register:				
• All cheques				
• Current period cheques only				
Manual cheques listing				
5.2. User Specified Reports				
Cheque				
Advice				
Debit/credit memo				
Produce dummy cheque for forms alignment				

Table 4
SOFTWARE REQUIREMENTS – RETAIL INVOICING

	Required		Available	
	Mandatory	**Desirable**	**#1**	**#2**
1. SYSTEM CAPACITY				
1.1. Maximum number of				
Items				
Categories				
Salespeople				
Credit cards				
Tax types				
Layaways on file				
Quotations on file				
2. DATA FILES				
2.1. Transaction Data				
Entry type				
Customer number				
Salesperson				
Reference				
Customer billing information				

Customer ship to information	______	______	______	______
Tax status	______	______	______	______
Invoice date	______	______	______	______
Ship date	______	______	______	______
Payment terms	______	______	______	______
Ship via method	______	______	______	______
Item code	______	______	______	______
Description	______	______	______	______
Price	______	______	______	______
Quantity	______	______	______	______
Extended amount	______	______	______	______
Item tax status	______	______	______	______
Tax exempt numbers	______	______	______	______

3. PROCESSING

3.1. Invoicing

Ability to process:				
• Invoices	______	______	______	______
• Credit notes	______	______	______	______
• Quotations	______	______	______	______
• Layaway/deposits	______	______	______	______
• Accounts receivable cash receipts	______	______	______	______
• Miscellaneous cash receipts	______	______	______	______
• Miscellaneous cash payments	______	______	______	______
Tax calculation:				
• Identify items as taxable:				
• all taxes	______	______	______	______
• specific taxes only (required for GST)	______	______	______	______
• Identify individuals as tax exempt	______	______	______	______
Online editing of:				
• Customer number	______	______	______	______
• Salesperson code	______	______	______	______
• Invoice date	______	______	______	______
• Ship date	______	______	______	______

3.2. Update Price List

Ability to update prices:				
• By range of item numbers	______	______	______	______
• By range of categories	______	______	______	______

- By costs ______ ______ ______ ______
- By percentage ______ ______ ______ ______
- By a fixed amount ______ ______ ______ ______
- Sale prices ______ ______ ______ ______

3.3. General

Ability to open cash drawer from screen ______ ______ ______ ______

Interface with:

- Accounts Receivable ______ ______ ______ ______
- Inventory Control ______ ______ ______ ______
- General Ledger ______ ______ ______ ______

Calculate commission:

- Sales ______ ______ ______ ______
- Gross margin ______ ______ ______ ______
- Varying rates by category ______ ______ ______ ______

4. INQUIRY

4.1. Quotations

Outstanding quotations:

- By customer ______ ______ ______ ______
- By quotation ______ ______ ______ ______

4.2. Layaways

Open layaways:

- By customer ______ ______ ______ ______
- By layaway ______ ______ ______ ______

4.3. Price File

Price lookup by:

- Item number ______ ______ ______ ______
- Description ______ ______ ______ ______

5. REPORTS

5.1. Standard Reports

Sales analysis:

- By category ______ ______ ______ ______
- By month ______ ______ ______ ______
- In detail ______ ______ ______ ______
- In summary ______ ______ ______ ______

Sales and commissions summary:

- By salesperson ______ ______ ______ ______

Price list:

- By item ______ ______ ______ ______

• By category	______	______	______	______
Quotation list:				
• By customer number	______	______	______	______
Layaway list:				
• By customer number	______	______	______	______
Daily reports:				
• Sales recap	______	______	______	______
• Sales summary by payment type	______	______	______	______
• Sales summary by category	______	______	______	______
• Sales summary by salesperson	______	______	______	______
• Commission by category	______	______	______	______
• Cash drawer log	______	______	______	______

Table 5
SOFTWARE REQUIREMENTS – INVENTORY CONTROL

	Required		Available	
	Mandatory	**Desirable**	**#1**	**#2**
1. SYSTEM CAPACITY				
1.1. Maximum number of				
Items	______	______	______	______
Segments in item number	______	______	______	______
Characters in item number	______	______	______	______
Locations	______	______	______	______
Alternative units per item	______	______	______	______
Serial numbers per item	______	______	______	______
Discount codes per item	______	______	______	______
Sales history periods	______	______	______	______
Levels of Bill of Materials	______	______	______	______
2. DATA FILES				
2.1. Item Record				
Item number	______	______	______	______
Brand	______	______	______	______
Style	______	______	______	______
Size	______	______	______	______
Colour	______	______	______	______
Season	______	______	______	______
Locations	______	______	______	______
Description	______	______	______	______

Category code	______	______	______	______
Stocking unit	______	______	______	______
Costing method	______	______	______	______
Base price	______	______	______	______
Five or more price levels	______	______	______	______
Fractional pricing	______	______	______	______
Sale price:				
• Sale date range	______	______	______	______
Commission type	______	______	______	______
Commission rate	______	______	______	______
Cost:				
• Standard	______	______	______	______
• Most recent	______	______	______	______
• Other	______	______	______	______
• Prior year average	______	______	______	______
Tax status	______	______	______	______
Picking sequence (bin number)	______	______	______	______
Stock item status	______	______	______	______
Alternative item number	______	______	______	______
Mark-up factor	______	______	______	______
Serial number	______	______	______	______
Unit weight	______	______	______	______
Alternative units of measure:				
• Whole unit conversion factor	______	______	______	______
• Decimals allowed in conversion factor	______	______	______	______
Pricing policy:				
• Based on discounts	______	______	______	______
• Based on mark-ups	______	______	______	______
Discount policy:				
• Based on percentage	______	______	______	______
• Based on amount	______	______	______	______
Pricing determined by:				
• Customer type	______	______	______	______
• Quantity purchased	______	______	______	______
Lowest authorized mark-down	______	______	______	______
Primary vendor	______	______	______	______
Alternative vendor	______	______	______	______
Vendor item number	______	______	______	______
Quantity:				
• On hand	______	______	______	______

- On order ______ ______ ______ ______
- Committed ______ ______ ______ ______
- Reserved ______ ______ ______ ______
- Available ______ ______ ______ ______

Stock levels:

- Minimum ______ ______ ______ ______
- Optimum ______ ______ ______ ______
- Maximum ______ ______ ______ ______
- Reorder point ______ ______ ______ ______
- Reorder quantity ______ ______ ______ ______
- Lead time ______ ______ ______ ______

Last receipt:

- Quantity ______ ______ ______ ______
- Date ______ ______ ______ ______

Last inventory adjustment:

- Quantity ______ ______ ______ ______
- Type ______ ______ ______ ______
- Date ______ ______ ______ ______

Last sale:

- Date ______ ______ ______ ______
- Price ______ ______ ______ ______

Sales history:

- Current day ______ ______ ______ ______
- Current week to date ______ ______ ______ ______
- Current month to date ______ ______ ______ ______
- Current year to date ______ ______ ______ ______
- Current season to date ______ ______ ______ ______
- Prior year month ______ ______ ______ ______
- Prior year quarter ______ ______ ______ ______
- Prior year ______ ______ ______ ______
- Quantity returned ______ ______ ______ ______

2.2. Transaction Records

Reference number ______ ______ ______ ______
Entry type ______ ______ ______ ______
Date ______ ______ ______ ______
Customer number ______ ______ ______ ______
Item number ______ ______ ______ ______
Category code ______ ______ ______ ______
Location code ______ ______ ______ ______
Quantity ______ ______ ______ ______

Unit price	______	______	______	______
Unit of measure	______	______	______	______

3. PROCESSING

3.1. Costing Method

Required costing method:

• Average	______	______	______	______
• Standard	______	______	______	______
• Last in first out	______	______	______	______
• First in first out	______	______	______	______
• Specific	______	______	______	______

3.2. Purchases/Receipts

Online edit for valid:

• Unique purchase order number	______	______	______	______
• Order date	______	______	______	______
• Vendor number	______	______	______	______
• Item number	______	______	______	______
• Location	______	______	______	______
• Unit of measure	______	______	______	______

Ability to review during purchase order entry:

• Quantity on hand	______	______	______	______
• Quantity on order	______	______	______	______
• Quantity on sales order	______	______	______	______
• By location	______	______	______	______
• In total	______	______	______	______
Print labels for items received	______	______	______	______
Ability to keep P.O. open until all goods received	______	______	______	______
Ability to calculate optimum stock level and reorder point	______	______	______	______
Suggested reorder quantity	______	______	______	______

3.3. Shipments

Online edit for valid:

• Date	______	______	______	______
• Customer number	______	______	______	______
• Item number	______	______	______	______
• Category code	______	______	______	______
• Location code	______	______	______	______

	Override unit price at shipping point	______	______	______	______
	Create negative quantities option	______	______	______	______
	Ability to process serial number information	______	______	______	______
3.4.	<u>Adjustments</u>				
	Online edit for valid:				
	• Date	______	______	______	______
	• Item number	______	______	______	______
	• Location	______	______	______	______
	Adjust for:				
	• Quantity	______	______	______	______
	• Cost	______	______	______	______
3.5.	<u>Stock Transfers</u>				
	Online edit for valid:				
	• Date	______	______	______	______
	• Item number	______	______	______	______
	• Location	______	______	______	______
	• Unit of measure	______	______	______	______
3.6.	<u>Bill of Material Assemblies</u>				
	Online edit of:				
	• Item number	______	______	______	______
	• Bill of Material number	______	______	______	______
	• Location code	______	______	______	______
	• Date	______	______	______	______
	Warning for items with insufficient quantities	______	______	______	______
	Automatic assembly of sub-assemblies	______	______	______	______
	Generate assemblies by:				
	• Item number	______	______	______	______
	• Range of item number	______	______	______	______
3.7.	<u>Stock Takes</u>				
	Create inventory worksheet:				
	• Multiple units of measure	______	______	______	______
	• By location	______	______	______	______
	• By picking sequence	______	______	______	______
	• By item number	______	______	______	______
	• Optional quantity on hand	______	______	______	______
	Entry of physical counts:				
	• Sorted by worksheet	______	______	______	______

- Item numbers pre-input from worksheet ______ ______ ______ ______
- Default to on-hand amount for fast entry ______ ______ ______ ______

Ability to interface with a hand-held device for counting stock ______ ______ ______ ______

3.8. General

Force audit trail before posting ______ ______ ______ ______

Force master file change report ______ ______ ______ ______

Interface with:

- Order Entry/Retail Invoicing ______ ______ ______ ______
- General Ledger ______ ______ ______ ______
- Job Costing ______ ______ ______ ______
- Cash register software ______ ______ ______ ______

Import from DOS-based software ______ ______ ______ ______

Capability to interface with Electronic Data Interchange systems ______ ______ ______ ______

Ability to purge inactive items by user-defined criteria ______ ______ ______ ______

Supports bar code reader ______ ______ ______ ______

Update price list:

- By category ______ ______ ______ ______
- By item number ______ ______ ______ ______
- By segment ______ ______ ______ ______
- By report group ______ ______ ______ ______
- By vendor ______ ______ ______ ______
- For base price ______ ______ ______ ______
- For stock price ______ ______ ______ ______
- By percentage ______ ______ ______ ______
- By amount ______ ______ ______ ______
- By mark-up ______ ______ ______ ______
- By margin ______ ______ ______ ______

Supports graphic analysis ______ ______ ______ ______

4. INQUIRY

4.1. Item Display

Display item by:

- Item number ______ ______ ______ ______
- Item description ______ ______ ______ ______

Alternative items				
Last shipment date				
Last receipt date				
Average days between shipments				
Average units shipped				
Quantities by:				
• Location				
• Bin location				
• Quantity on hand				
• Quantity on purchase order				
• Quantity on sales order				
Units of measure information				
Pricing policy				
Vendor information				
Purchase order information:				
• Location				
• Purchase order number				
• Vendor				
• Quantity on purchase order				
• Quantity received				
• Expected date				
Costs:				
• Standard cost				
• Most recent cost				
• Other				
• Average unit cost				
Reorder date:				
• Minimum level				
• Maximum level				
• Reorder quantity				
Sales history:				
• Quantity sold				
• Sales amount				
• Actual cost				
• By period				
• Year to date				
• Prior year				
4.2. Bill of Material Information				
Component item numbers				
Quantity				

Fixed cost ______ ______ ______ ______
Variable cost ______ ______ ______ ______

5. REPORTING

5.1. Standard Reports

Item status

Item valuation report: ______ ______ ______ ______
- By location ______ ______ ______ ______
- In detail ______ ______ ______ ______
- In summary ______ ______ ______ ______
- Actual cost ______ ______ ______ ______
- Most recent cost ______ ______ ______ ______
- Selling price ______ ______ ______ ______
- Standard cost ______ ______ ______ ______
- Other cost ______ ______ ______ ______
- By item number ______ ______ ______ ______
- By item segment ______ ______ ______ ______
- By category ______ ______ ______ ______
- By report group ______ ______ ______ ______

Overstocked items report:
- By item number ______ ______ ______ ______
- By segment ______ ______ ______ ______
- By category ______ ______ ______ ______
- By report group ______ ______ ______ ______
- By location ______ ______ ______ ______

Reorder report:
- By category code ______ ______ ______ ______
- By item number ______ ______ ______ ______
- By item segment ______ ______ ______ ______
- By report group ______ ______ ______ ______
- By vendor ______ ______ ______ ______
- By location ______ ______ ______ ______

Slow-moving items:
- By category ______ ______ ______ ______
- By item number ______ ______ ______ ______
- By segment ______ ______ ______ ______
- By report group ______ ______ ______ ______
- By period:
  - current period ______ ______ ______ ______
  - year to date ______ ______ ______ ______

Purchase orders and receipts:

• By purchase order number	______	______	______	______
• By expected receipt date	______	______	______	______
Transaction history:				
• By category	______	______	______	______
• By date	______	______	______	______
• By item number	______	______	______	______
• By segment	______	______	______	______
• By location	______	______	______	______
• By reference	______	______	______	______
• By source	______	______	______	______
• By transaction type	______	______	______	______
Price list:				
• By category	______	______	______	______
• By item	______	______	______	______
• By segment	______	______	______	______
• By report groups	______	______	______	______
• By location	______	______	______	______
• By vendor	______	______	______	______
Margin analysis:				
• By category	______	______	______	______
• By item number	______	______	______	______
• By segment	______	______	______	______
• By report group	______	______	______	______
• For user-specified margin using:				
• average cost	______	______	______	______
• most recent cost	______	______	______	______
• standard cost	______	______	______	______
• other cost	______	______	______	______
Mark-up analysis:				
• By category	______	______	______	______
• By item number	______	______	______	______
• By segment	______	______	______	______
• By report	______	______	______	______
• For user-specified mark-up based on:				
• most recent cost	______	______	______	______
• standard cost	______	______	______	______
• other	______	______	______	______
Sales history:				
• By category	______	______	______	______
• By item	______	______	______	______
• By segment	______	______	______	______

• By report group	______	______	______	______
• In summary	______	______	______	______
• In detail	______	______	______	______
Summary sales statistics	______	______	______	______
Price change report	______	______	______	______
Turnover analysis:				
• By current sales	______	______	______	______
• By historical sales	______	______	______	______
• By budget sales	______	______	______	______
• Year to date	______	______	______	______
• Period to date	______	______	______	______
Inventory ageing reports	______	______	______	______
Suggested transfer report:				
• By user-specified percentage	______	______	______	______
5.2. <u>User-Defined Reports</u>				
Bin and item labels	______	______	______	______
Custom reports from data files	______	______	______	______

INDEX